OPTIONS TRADING FOR

BEGINNERS

THE BEST DAY TRADING CRASH COURSE WITH BASIC
STRATEGIES FOR INVESTING IN THE STOCK MARKET

TABLE OF CONTENTS

3

Introduction

Financial Freedom

Many people seek it but few have it. That is because the secrets behind obtaining it are closely guarded by those who have it. This book is about exposing one true and reliable way that you can earn the financial security and independence you need to take control of the way you live your daily life.

Signs of Financial Slavery

The first active step needed to get started on a journey to financial freedom is acknowledging that you are not financially stable or free. This is a hard pill for some people to swallow and so, they avoid acknowledging it even with the overwhelming evidence to support the state.

Facing this fact is not about demeaning your integrity or bring you down. It is about giving you a foundation to start with so that you can build the financial security you need. This knowledge is needed to show you where you currently stand financially and what your resources are so that you can develop a plan to get where you need and want to be.

The following conditions are those that chain many people to financial slavery:

- **Living Paycheck to Paycheck.** People who live this way do not have an emergency fund and typically have accompanying credit card debt because they need to subsidize their expenses, which are higher than their income. Many people live this way. In fact, more than 40% of American households could not cover a $400 expense such as medical bills or car repairs if it came up unexpectedly in 2017.

- **Not Having Enough Saved Up to Sustain Their Lifestyle if They Were to Lose Their Job.** People such as these do not have enough money accumulated to take time away from working daily. This is the reason why most people are in careers and jobs that bring them no joy. They need the salary to keep a roof over their heads and food in their belly and so, they deal with the circumstances that make them unhappy.

- **Not being able to pursue the activities and adventures that bring happiness while still saving and accumulating wealth.** These types of people are stuck in a cycle of trading their daily hours for money while still being unable to enjoy the money that they earn because it is not enough to allow them this enjoyment and still pay the bills.

- **Having inflexible schedules**. Most people are stuck in a cycle of working every day and going home to come back to work the next day. Therefore, they have to give this time to earn an income and become chained to their jobs.

- **Not being able to retire comfortably at the desired age.** The world over, the average age for retirement is 65 years old. However, many people are not expected to live even 20 years past that age. That does not leave much time to enjoy a life free of accumulating wealth. The sadder fact is that most people do not retire with enough money saved up to enjoy the things that they want after retirement. Others still have to work a job even after this age to sustain themselves. People financially free can retire at the age that they want rather than one that is dictated by someone else. They also have the capital available to do the things they want to do and still have income coming to them on a more passive basis.

- **Spending more money than earned**. This results because people want to live the lifestyle that they want, but cannot afford, or people needing to subsidize their income to cater to their needs. To build wealth, you cannot have more money going out than coming in. Signs that your spending exceeds your income include having a budget based on your salary, having an expense list that exceeds your net income, carrying a balance on your credit card, having rent or mortgage that is more than 30% of your net income and buying things to impress or keep up with other people.

Are you a slave to your finances? Would you like to use your time in other ways while still earning a steady and growing income? Can you use an extra income to develop the lifestyle you want?

If your answer is yes to any of these income questions or relating to even just one of the conditions stated above, means you can use the advice and strategies outlined in this book.

Financial Freedom — What Is It and Why Do Only A Few People Have It?

Having financial freedom is more than just having a 6-month emergency fund saved up and your debt cleared. Financial freedom means taking control of your time and finances so that you can do the things that you want to do rather than what your bank account figure dictates. Being financially free means that you do not need to trade your time for money.

To be able to gain this financial freedom, you need to have financial security. Financial security is the condition whereby you support the standard of living you want now and in the future by having stable sources of income and other resources available to you. That means not living paycheck to paycheck. It means not having to worry about where your next dollar will come from. It means having a huge weight lifted off your shoulders because you know there are resources you can leverage to get the things that you want and need.

People who have financial freedom are also financially independent. Financial independence is the state of having personal wealth to maintain the lifestyle and the standard of living you want without actually having to trade your daily hours for money. The assets and resources you have generated will gain that income for you, so that your income remains far greater than your expenses. In essence, being financially independent means you can go for a prolonged period without trading time for money and still have the standard of living that you want. That you can go on a yearlong vacation and still be secure in the knowledge that your wealth is still growing.

To be financially independent, you have to have:

- An emergency fund that can sustain your lifestyle for an extended period (years).

- Assets that produce income for you on a daily, weekly, monthly, and yearly basis.

- Very little or zero debt.

Very few people on the planet are financially secure and independent. In fact, more than 1 billion people live in extreme poverty. In 2015, it was estimated that more than 10% of the global population lived on less than US$1.90 per day.

Despite these statistics, there is hope. This hope comes from the fact that this statistic goes down every year. In fact, in 2019 less than 8% of the global population lived in extreme poverty. This is largely attributed to the fact that people being more educated about their options and are not just accepting of these poor circumstances.

Despite this improvement, most of the global population still trades their time for an hourly wage. The income earned from this is not sustainable nor will it allow them to live the standard of life that they would like. They will not be able to retire comfortably. There is no power or security in living this way.

People who are financially free have learned and harnessed the power of passive income. Passive income is wealth that is generated from little to no effort or earned in the way of exchanging time for money over the long term. While it might take a massive amount of time and effort to establish in the beginning, passive income allows you to earn money even while you sleep with little to no daily effort required for its maintenance.

The beauty of passive income is that it is not only limited to one income bracket or portion of the population. Anyone can develop passive income as long as they develop the right mindset and is willing to put in the time and effort to learn and be consistent in pursuing this standard of living.

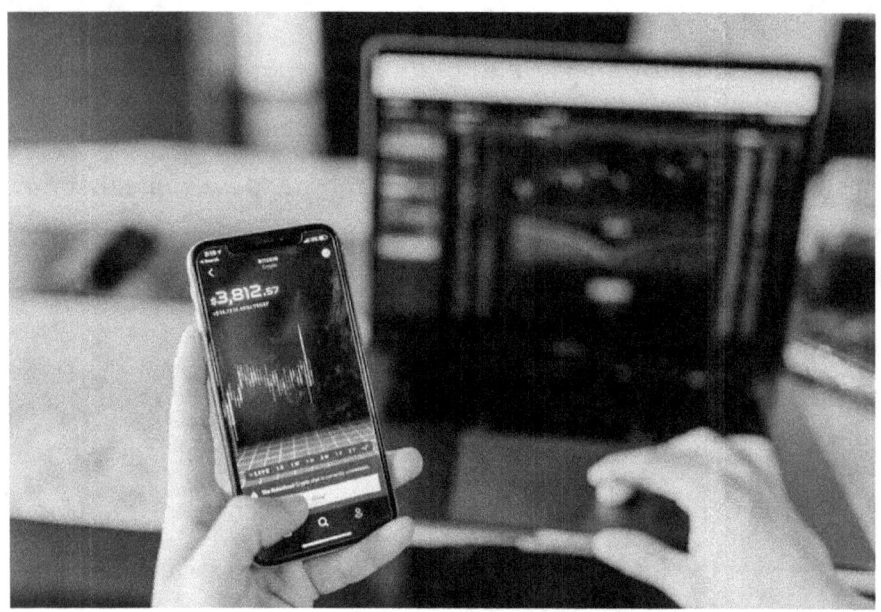

Chapter 1. Options Trading Basics

There are many choices available when it comes to earning passive income and developing a strategy to gain financial freedom. Investing in real estate and trading stock are common contenders. However, options trading is incomparable in terms of its affordability and accessibility.

Trading options is a powerful way of gaining financial freedom whatever it may mean to you. This is not a job that you have to show up to from 9 to 5 to benefit greatly from it. While there is some upfront human and monetary capital to be invested, once you get your feet wet, you will see the trading options are rather easy with the knowledge and experience under your belt. Next to real estate and stock trading, options trading is one of the most powerful ways to gain financial freedom passively.

Derivative Contract

The option derives its value based on the value of the underlying asset, hence the term derivative contract. Derivative contracts are often used for commodities like gold, oil, and currencies, which are often in the form of US dollars. Another type of derivative is based on the value of stocks and bonds. They can also be based on interest rates such as the yield on a specified amount of time Treasury note, as a 10-year Treasury note.

In a derivative contract, the seller does not have to own the specified asset. All they have to do is have enough money to cover the price of the asset to fulfill the contract. The seller also has the option of giving the buyer another derivative contract to offset the asset's value. These choices are often practiced because they are easier than providing the asset itself.

Options vs. Stocks

Trading options and trading stocks are different because stocks and options have different characteristics. Stocks represent shares of ownership in individual companies or options. This allows the stock trader to bet in any direction that they feel the stock price is headed.

Stocks are a great investment if you are thinking of long-term yield such as for retirement and have the capital. They are very simplistic in the approach in which the trader buys the stock and wagers on the price that he or she thinks it will rise at a certain time in the future. The hope is that the price will increase in value, thus gaining the trader a substantial yield.

Stocks are also a great option for those who want to invest without having to keep a steady eye on the growth of the investment.

The risk of investing in stocks is that the price of stocks can plummet to zero at any moment. This means that the investor can lose his or her entire investment at the drop of a hat because stocks are very volatile from day to day. They are very reactive to world events such as wars, politics, scandals, epidemics, and natural disasters.

On the other hand, options are a great option for traders who would like flexibility with timing and risks. The trader is under no obligation and can see how the trade plays out over the time specified by the option contract. In that period the price is locked, which is also a great appeal.

Trading options also require a lower investment compared to stocks typically.

Another great appeal for options reading is that the specified period is typically shorter than investing in stocks. This allows for regular buying and selling as options have different expiration dates. Expiration dates can range from just a few days to several years.

The drawback that makes some people hesitate in trading options is that it is more complex than trading stocks. The trader needs to learn new jargon and vocabulary such as strike prices, calls, and puts so that they can determine how to set up effective options. Not only does the trader have to learn new terms, but he or she also has to develop new skillsets and the right mindset for options trading.

Benefits of Trading Options

There are several advantages to trading options and they include:

- **The initial investment is lower than with trading stocks.** This means that the options trader can benefit from playing in the same financial market as a stock trader without paying as much upfront. This is called hedging.

- **The options trader is not required to own the asset to benefit from its value.** This means that the trader does not incur the cost associated with the asset. Costs can include transportation and storage fees if applicable.

- **There is no obligation to follow through with the transaction**. Whether the trader is exercising a call or put option, at the end of the day, the loss is limited because the trader is only obligated to pay for the contract and nothing more. Only if the trader feels it is worthwhile, does he or she take steps to proceed with the exercise of the contract.

- **The options trader has many choices.** Trading options gives the trader great flexibility. Traders can choose to:

  - Sell the options to another investor in the case of in the money situations.

  - Exercise the contract and buy the asset.

- Exercise the option and sell all or part of the asset.

- In the case of out of the money situations, sell the options to another investor before the expiration date arrives.

- **The strike price freezes the price.** This allows the options trader the ability to buy or sell the asset on or before the expiration date without the worry of fluctuating prices.

- **Options can protect an asset from depreciating market prices.** This long-term strategy can protect assets from drops in the price market. Exercising a call allows the trader to buy the asset at a lower price.

- **The trader can earn passive income from assets that he or she already owns.** You can sell call options on your own assets to earn income through traders paying you premiums.

Tips for Getting Started with Options Trading

Develop a Trading Plan before Getting Started

You need this plan to develop consistency in your actions when it comes to trading options. This will tell you how you will trade, the money you will allocate to trading, and define how you will track your performance. Doing this will also allow you to understand the risks involved in options, so that you can plan ahead to minimize them.

Practicing How to Earn a Profit from Options Trading On Paper First Before Investing Actual Money

This is called paper trading and it prevents you from risking your hard-earned cash before you know what you are doing. This is done a few weeks to a few months before you do the real thing. Use spreadsheets or any other tools that make it easy for you to enter practice trades, so that you can evaluate their performance over the time set for expiration. The benefits of doing this include taking away the psychological pressure of learning the mechanics without actually trading your own money.

Open a Brokerage Account

This can be done in 2 ways—through online websites or more traditionally through a broker. This is something you need to consider carefully. Things that need to be considered include:

- The reputation of the brokerage firm. Be sure to look out for scams, which can be especially prevalent online.

- The commissions that the brokerage firm charges. If you are lucky, you might even find a firm that does not charge commissions on options.

- Be aware of the types of accounts that you need. They include a cash account and a margin account. A cash account is one that is loaded with cash to facilitate the buying of options. On the other hand, margin accounts allow the trader to borrow money against the value of the securities in the trader's account.

- If you choose to trade options online, be sure that the brokerage firm accepts safe payment methods like a secure credit card payment gateway, PayPal, Payoneer, etc.

- Ensure that you are approved to trade options. This can be done through your brokerage firm.

Choose a Trading Style

There are two main types of options traders. The two categories of traders are professional traders (traders that work on behalf of institutions and clients) and individual traders who trade strictly for themselves. Both of these types of traders pick from the same pool of trading styles whether or not they are trading for themselves or someone else. The different trading styles include:

- **Day trading.** Full-time options traders use this method. It is more largely used by professional options traders. It involves constantly monitoring the financial markets. The name comes from the fact that the trades do not last more than a day. Profits, losses, or breakeven are realized by the end of the day and so the options are closed.

- **Position trading.** This is a low-maintenance style that introduces low risk, but requires an advanced trader's knowledge and understanding of options and the financial markets. It is mainly used by professionals.

- **Swing trading.** This style of options trading is particularly useful for part-time trading as well as beginners who are just getting the hang of things.

- **Market makers.** This is done in a professional capacity. Market makers are the ones who ensure that the market is liquid and has transactions to be engaged in. Without market makers, there will a low volume of options to be transacted and the trades market would be stagnant.

Never Invest Money You Cannot Afford or Are Not Willing to Lose

Investing is a technique used to make your money work for you. When it is done right, the investor will receive more money than he or she started with. However, jumping the gun can lead to losses because investing is a risk. There is no guarantee that your money will compound itself. In fact, you may lose the entire investment. That is why you should never put-up money you cannot afford to do without investing. To avoid do this, be patient, do not be greedy, and keep your costs as low as possible.

Never Invest All Your Resources in One Option

This embodies the saying, "Never keep all your eggs in one basket." Remember that investing in options is a risk. Spread that risk by not limiting yourself to one option.

Never tie up all your capital in options trades. This goes back to keeping your options open. Sustainable income should never come from one place. Ensure doing other things to build your wealth and not solely reliant on options. Diversify your options portfolio, so that not all your eggs are in the same basket.

Know Your Breakeven Points

Breakeven describes the point at which total income equals the total. We will discuss this further as we delve into options trading strategies.

Do your research before investing in options. Always.

Anticipate losses and plan for them.

If you have at least 5 losing trades back-to-back, stop and go back to the drawing board to discover what you are doing wrong and how you can rectify this. Evaluate continuously your strategies to discover shortfalls.

Have an exit strategy for each option and know when to implement this strategy.

Join Online Forums So That You Can Learn from Other Options Traders

This can be a valuable resource of support, information, and development of technique. This is also a place you can learn from the successes and failures of other options traders so that you do not have to repeat the failures and you can use the success stories to advance your options.

Chapter 2. What Is an Option Contract?

An option contract has three elements to it: the strike price, the option type, and the expiry date. The strike price is not to be confused with the option contract price. The strike is simply the level beyond which the option comes 'into the money.' This is best explained via an example.

If you buy a call option for a stock, say AAPL, with a strike price of $160, this means you can buy the underlying stock at any time before its expiry. Since you've bought a call option, ideally you want the stock's market price to be greater than the strike price. This way, you can buy the stock at the lower option strike price and sell it at the higher market price. Thus, the call option is in the money in such a scenario.

For a put, on the other hand, you can only make money when the underlying market price is lower than the option's strike price. So, if you purchased an AAPL put with a strike price of $160, you can only make money when the stock is trading for less than $160. It is only in this scenario that the put is in the money. Hence, the strike price is the price, which the market price must cross; the direction depends on whether the option is a call or a put for you to make money on the option.

Next up is the expiry date. Options contracts don't exist forever, they expire at certain periods. The most common expiry date for an option is the last trading day of a month. Options usually exist for month-long periods, although there are some cases where they may exist for longer periods, sometimes years. These longer options are called LEAPS and are not the subject of our discussion in this book.

When you pull up quotes for an options contract in your broker's terminal, you will usually see contracts for three expiry dates: the current month, the next month (near month), and the month after that (the far month). Trading volumes are the greatest for current and near month options, with near month volumes gradually increasing as the current month's expiry date draws closer.

As the name, expiry date, suggests, the contract is not valid beyond this date and must be exercised either on or before this date. This brings us to the type of option. There are two types available: American and European. American options are more widely available and are preferred as trading instruments because they can be exercised on any day before the expiry date.

By contrast, European options can be exercised only on the expiry date and not prior, and not after. As you can imagine, this isn't very ideal for a trader since your chances of being right are greater over some time, like with the American option, as opposed to a day.

The next thing you ought to familiarize yourself with is the option contract ticker. The ticker for a contract is an amalgam of information so let's break this down. I'm going to use an actual example here:

AAPL190607C00150000 is an option that is currently trading at $25.60 with a strike price of 150$ and expiring on June 7th. This is a call option. Here's how this is broken down:

AAPL-this is the underlying stock's symbol, in this case, Apple Inc.

190607-this is the expiry date listed in yy/mm/dd format. Hence, June 7th, 2019.

C-This indicates this is a call option. A put would be denoted by a P.

00150000-This is the strike price represented as five digits before the decimal and three after. In this case, it is 00150.000 or $150.

Similarly, AAPL190607P00145000 is a put option on AAPL, expiring on 7th June 2019, with a strike price of $145.

Options are generally a lot different compared to most other financial securities like stocks, commodities, bonds, and currencies. The value of an options contract depends upon the value of the underlying asset. As such, options are ideally contracts permitting future transactions based on the underlying security. Two parties consisting of a buyer and a seller enter the contract.

The contracts come with terms relevant to future transactions. For instance, there is always a definition of the underlying asset and its properties. For instance, the contract will define the underlying security, the price, expiration date, and if it can be sold or purchased.

Investors have plenty of financial and strategic leeway with options compared to simply investing in stocks. By investing in options, traders not only hedge to protect against losses but also gain access to stocks at a fraction of the normal costs. Options contracts lower your risk in all market conditions on speculative bets and increase your profits on any new or existing positions you may take.

Trading in options has a lot of positives compared to trading in stocks only or other securities. However, there are some inherent risks that you need to be aware of. As a potential trader, you need to be aware of the great benefits as well as inherent risks relating to trading options.

There are various standardized components of option contracting that enable ease in engaging in options trading. These components characterize the mechanics of how options trading binds the parties involved and demonstrates the way profits can be generated if the market forces are favorable.

Among the components of options trading are:

Underlying Securities

Options that are traded on the market only apply to certain assets. These assets are then referred to as underlying securities. Some companies provide the asset against which the option operators list options. ASX is one operator in the options trading market that has played a key role in the listing of underlying securities.

The term classes of options refer to the listing of puts and calls as options of the same assets. An example is when puts and calls are applied to a lease corporation's shares. This does not put in regarding the contract terms in terms of the predetermined price or duration of the expiry of the call and put contracts. An operator of options trading usually provides the list of the available classes for the benefit of investors.

Contract Size

On the ASX platform of options trading, the market standardizes the size of the option contract at 100 underlying securities. Therefore, one option contract corresponds to 100 underlying shares. The changes that can happen only come when reorganization happens on the initial outlay of the underlying share or the capital therein. Index options usually fix the value of the contract at a certain stipulated dollar rate.

Expiry Day

Options are constrained by time and have a life span. There are predetermined expiry deadlines that the platform operator sets that have to be respected. These deadlines are usually rigid, and once they are out the rights under a contract in a particular class of unexercised options are then forfeited. Usually, the last day of the life span of a contract is the summative trading date. For shares that have their expiry coming by June of 2020, the options over them have their last trading day on a Thursday that comes before the last Friday that happens to be in the month. Those that expire beyond June 2020, expiry is on the third Thursday that happens to be in the month. For index options. Expiries come on the concurrent third Thursday of the same month of writing the option. However, these dates can be readjusted by the options platform operator as and when there is a reason for such action.

In recent years, platform operators have introduced more short-term options for some underlying. Some are weekly, while others are on a fortnightly basis. These have the corresponding weekly or fortnightly expiries. When the lifespan of options runs out, the operators then create new deadlines. However, all classes of options have their expiries subject to quarters of the financial calendar.

Exercise Prices

These are the buying price or the price of selling the assets or underlying securities. These prices are also called strike prices. They are usually predetermined in the option contract and have to be met if one has to exercise the rights in an option. Essentially, they are called exercise because the parties are now invoking the rights that are stipulated in an option to either buy or sell. Therefore, the exercise of the option is subject to the price stipulations.

The platform operator usually predetermines the prices. Various prices can be listed as available on the market for the same expiry of a certain class of options. Usually, prices depend on the value of the underlying share value. If the value of the underlying prices increases, the exercise prices also increase commensurately. The need to offer a range of prices for the same option contract is to suit the market conveniences of buyers of the contracts. The buyer can better match their expectations of the pricing of the underlying shares given the position of their option contract. The exercise prices can also be varied in the course of an active contract when market dynamics dictate that such a move has to be made.

Adjustments to Option Contracts

There is a general effort to ensure that option contracts are entered under conditions that are standardized to the greatest extent possible. However, some market forces may upset the set optimum conditions and specifications. This may call for the making of some adjustments to ensure the preservation of the value attached to the positions of the various options contracts that have been entered into by various takers and writers.

In making the adjustments, it has to be established the kind of upset that has been caused on the market. Usually, it may affect one or more components of the options market. Identifying the affected components is necessary so that the adjustment is specific and particular to the kind of area of trading affected.

ASX, as one of the platform operators, has its rules that try to retain a tentatively predictable and standardized environment of trade. However, it also provides guidelines for the kind of measures that have to be made when adjustments are required. Conventions that guide the process of adjustment cushion participants on this kind of market and protect takers and writers from arbitrary actions that may be unfavorable.

Chapter 3. Types of Trading Option

Options come in two major types—put options and call options. Traders choose the kind of option to trade-in depending on whether they want to buy or sell on the options market.

Call Options

The call option options make it possible for you to purchase an underlying asset associated with the option in question. When a call option is in the money, the bid or strike price is less in value than the underlying stock price. Traders always buy a call option when there is a possibility of its stock price to increase beyond the current bid price before the expiration is obtained. When this happens, the trader derives some profit from the call transaction.

Individuals who purchase call options are always known as holders. Once they acquire the option, they can sell it any time before the expiration date. The profit of any option is obtained by subtracting the strike price, premium, and transaction fees from the stock price. The resulting amount is what is called the intrinsic value. This difference is always a negative value when the trader has made a loss and zero value when no profit or loss has been realized.

The maximum amount that a trader can lose from an option is equivalent to its premium. This explains why most people purchase options and not the underlying security.

The call option comprises three components—the strike price, the premium, and the exercise or expiration date. The premium is the amount of money that a trader pays when acquiring a particular option. For instance, a trader may purchase a call option with $55 as the strike price, $5 premium, and an expiration period of one month; it means that you will pay the seller $5 as a premium. If the expiration date is reached before you exercise the option, you will only pay the $5. If, let's say, a week, the price goes up to $70, and you decide to sell your option, you will make a profit of $15 from the transaction less $5 paid as the premium. If the price goes below $55, you make a loss.

Investors may also decide to sell a call option when they are anticipating a decline in the stock price. As the stock price falls to a level that is lower than the strike price, the investor will get some profit from the transaction. The person selling a call is known as the writer of the call. He/she is the one with the obligation to sell shares to a buyer at a price determined beforehand.

Put Options

This grants you the ability to write or sell an asset or security at a cost that is already predetermined, also the expiration date. Both call and put options can be used on stocks, commodities, currencies, and indexes as underlying securities. In this case, the strike price becomes the cost by which you sell the option.

A put option allows you to sell a certain asset at a known cost and expiration date. This option can be used on a good number of underlying assets, including indexes, currencies, commodities, and stocks. The price at which a trader sells an option is called the strike price.

Traders make a profit from selling a put option when anticipating a decline in the strike price. They make a loss when the value of the stock increases to a level that is beyond the strike price. This indicates that the cost of a put option may rise or fall as time elapses.

A put option's intrinsic value can be derived by obtaining the difference in prices for the stock and the option. The resultant value keeps changing as the time value reduces in strength. When a stock option bears a positive intrinsic value, you say that it is in the money. A negative value of this shows that the option has fallen out of the money.

Similar to call options, you do not need to wait for your put options to expire before you exercise them. Since an option's premium value keeps varying with the stock price or the cost of any other underlying asset, you must exercise your options just at the right time to avoid incurring losses in the future.

Chapter 4. Volatility

A very important aspect that affects the majority of types of trading, is volatility. Volatility is common in the trading of options as well. Anything tends to have a drastic change or fluctuate. In investment terms, it is linked to the price rate of any kind of trading instrument that tends to move up and down. A financial instrument that comes along with a not so stable price rate is termed to have low volatility. On the contrary, a financial instrument that makes sharp movements in the price rate in any fixed direction is termed to have high volatility. You can measure the volatility of the markets of financing as well. When it is very tough to predict properly the condition of a market and the concerned prices tend to have rapid change daily, the market is called to be volatile in nature.

In the world of options trading, volatility plays a very important role as it comes with the power of imparting some effects on the price of the option. The majority of beginner traders cannot understand the related signs to volatility properly. This ultimately results in the development of huge problems. You won't be able to be a successful options trader without having proper knowledge about the volatility of the market.

Understanding Volatility

Volatility is the rate of the speed and amount related to changes. In the world of financing, it is the rate of the price movement of any financial instrument. Before starting with trade of any kind, it is important to gain proper knowledge about the price of the related instrument. You are also required to know the rate by which the price is most likely to change. It is a very useful tool, as with the help of volatility, you can determine the price of any trading instrument in the future. While talking about options trading, two main types of volatility are taken to be important. The first one is the historical volatility, which determines the volatility of the past. In short, it helps in determining the changes in price that happened in the past over a certain period. The second one is the implied volatility, which projects the price changes in the future.

Historical Volatility

It is also known as statistical volatility. It helps in determining the price changes of the underlying security. It finds out the speed at which the price of the underlying security has moved. So, the higher the value of statistical volatility, the more has been the price movement for the underlying assets. The price movement is determined for a particular period. Theoretically, when the value of SV is higher, it indicates that the underlying asset's price has a high chance to have some significant movement in the upcoming days. However, it only indicates a price movement of the future and does not guarantee anything.

One thing that you should always keep in mind regarding statistical volatility is that it is incapable of providing an insight into which particular direction the price will move. When the SV is high, it indicates that the security price has been rapidly moving up and down over a certain time. However, it also indicates that the current price might not have gone too far from the actual price. Similarly, when the value of SV is low, it indicates that there hasn't been much movement in the price of the security. But, it might be making a steady move in one direction at a particular speed.

The investors use SV for having a clear idea about the price change of the underlying asset, which relies on the changing speed of the past. There is no need to find out the present trend.

Implied Volatility

It is also known as projected volatility. Implied volatility is called IV in short. It is the volatility estimate of the future days for any underlying security. It is the projection of the speed along with the price of any underlying security that is most likely to move. The majority of traders are concerned about the total profit in addition to the time that is left until the expiry date as the prime factors for determining the option price. However, IV also acts as a very important factor in determining the option price. IV is calculated by considering various factors: the price of the underlying security, option's strike price, time left until the expiry date, statistical volatility, along with the current interest rate.

Since IV helps to indicate the price movement of an underlying asset, the price will be higher when the value of implied volatility is also higher. The main reason behind this is that for generating some potential profit, the underlying asset's price needs to show some drastic movement in price.

Chapter 5. Option Pricing Models

Here are a few pricing models to adopt when trying to find out the price of an option. All you have to do is thoroughly understand a few good templates and then use an online calculator.

Model of the Black-Scholes

In 1973, Robert Merton, Myron Paddy, and Fischer Black developed the Black-Scholes pricing model as a means of premium computing options. This model has been the most famous since then. In reality, Merton and Paddy won the Nobel Prize in Economics two years after Black died in 1995. However, Black was still remembered for his role, although he did not receive the Nobel Prize because it is only awarded to living people.

The Black-Scholes model applies only to European options, both put and call and does not include paid dividends in its estimation. However, the use of the ex-dividend value of the asset can also be used.

The model assumes that the option can only be exercised when it expires, and that's why only European options are being considered.

Moreover, apart from not accepting paid dividends, this model also does not take into account any commissions.

It also implies that the market is effective and that market fluctuations are not predictable. Volatility and risk-free interest rates are stable and well known. Finally, the Black-Scholes model assumes that returns are normally distributed.

This option only takes into account one risky asset, such as a stock, and then a risk-free asset, such as cash. There is no possibility of arbitration for this, but there is a way for someone to borrow money at a risk-free rate with this model. You can also purchase any stock with this model, even a fraction of it, without any secret fees or costs. With this option, the derivatives are calculated at the present time, as well as the payoff. You can make a long stock investment with a short investment option.

In order to determine the option value, the Black-Scholes model includes the following:

- Risk-free interest rate.

- Implicit volatility.

- Time (expressed as a percentage of the year).

- The strike price.

- The current price of the underlying asset.

The formula for mathematics is complex. The average person will be frightened by using it. Luckily, online calculators are available that can be used to measure the price using this model. In addition, there are analytical instruments offered by trading platforms that are used to determine the price.

This is a decent way to get an investment approximation, but it's not the only way you're supposed to be depending on. Owing to market volatility, liquidity threats, and unexpected shifts and risks, you could be exposed to some big risks. There are also extreme price shifts, and much of the time, money doesn't come with an unchanging value in the real world. It's a good way to get a sense of what you're about to do, but at the same time, you're not supposed to rely on that.

Cox-Rubinstein Binomial Option Price Model

The version of the Black-Scholes model, the Cox-Ross-Rubenstein model, was developed by Mark Edward Rubenstein, Stephen Ross, and Carrington Cox. The primary advantage of this approach is that it uses a lattice-based model, which takes into account the price fluctuations of the underlying asset over time. The lattice-based model takes into account changes in various variables over the existence of the option. As a result, the price of the option is more accurate. It looks like a tree and progresses to the expiration of the stock in this way.

This model is being used for American options. It assumes that everyone is oblivious to risk, so that returns are equal to a risk-free interest rate.

The Cox-Ross-Rubenstein model often suggests that arbitration is not feasible because the market is perfectly efficient. The price of the underlying asset will never rise and fall at the same time. At any given time, it can only go in one direction. During the life of the option, different time points may be defined. It is also possible to establish a binomial tree.

Normally, this is determined from the beginning of the option to the end of the option, and then back again. When this has been achieved, it will be measured on the basis of the parameters of the changes in dividend rates, along with the changes in option prices. All of this is measured together and put into a statistical model to help others understand where their money is going.

The greatest advantage of this is that it works with American stocks. Another advantage is that it also allows you to see exactly where the stock is at a given stage. You can take a look at this, and through the analytical properties of this stock, you'll know where it will be in the future. In that respect, it's beneficial.

However, the greatest drawback is that it will take forever to calculate. You're looking at a lot of numbers all at the same time, and many older machines can't do it. However, with the advances in technology, the software is able to keep up with the pace of changing numbers. It's a smart idea to get an online calculator to see where the stock will be at a certain point in time.

Like the Cox-Ross-Rubenstein model, online pricing calculators and analytics tools offered by trading platforms can be used to know the option price.

The Parity of Put/Call

Hans Stoll introduced the put/call parity in 1969 as a pricing principle. According to his report, there is a connection between a European call and options with a similar strike price and an expiry date.

This means that for each call option value at a specific strike price, there is an appropriate put option value for that call option. The same goes for the fixed value of the option. There is an acceptable call option value for the specified put option value at a particular strike price. The relationship occurs because a position is formed, which is the same position as the underlying asset when there is a combination of call and call options.

The returns must be identical to the underlying asset and the option such that the arbitrage does not occur. Traders and investors who take advantage of arbitration can make a profit if the opportunity occurs.

The put/call parity is used to assess pricing models for European options. If the outcome of the pricing model does not satisfy a parity check, this means that arbitration will take place, and the model must be rejected as a pricing strategy. There are a variety of ways to measure the put/call parity.

Luckily, several trading platforms offer analytics software. These include visualizations of parity between put and call.

But of course, you don't have to memorize all the pricing models in full. Only choose one that suits your situation, have a simple online pricing model calculator, and let the numbers shift for you.

Chapter 6. Understanding How Options Are Priced

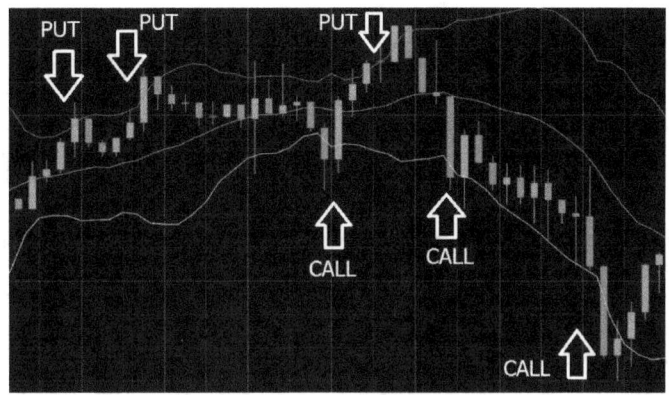

Time Value

The amount of time that an option has until it expires is directly related to how likely that same option will ultimately end in a profit greater than the intrinsic value before things are said and done. To determine the amount of time value that the option you are considering currently offers you will want to find the current price of the option and subtract from it the amount of intrinsic value that the same option currently has. It is common for options to hold onto 70 percent of their total value, or more, during the first half of their life before losing value much more rapidly after that point. It is also important to note that time value can change dramatically based on the volatility of the underlying asset both in the moment and based on its expectations in the future. As a general rule, the lower the time value, the more stable the option is likely to be.

Volatility

This is the measure of how swiftly and extensively the price of an underlying asset jumps up and down. Generally, the most profitable options contracts are volatile. The more frequent and extensive the oscillations, the more likely the option's price will go up. Even the slightest change in the estimated volatility can have a large impact on the premium. A shrewd trader should take the time to research the financial securities that are significantly volatile so that they can maximize their earning potential. The price oscillations of an underlying asset in the recent past are used to determine the premium. If the market takes over and the oscillations happen from moment to moment, then you have a case of implied volatility.

Dividends

When a trader fails to receive their dividend, the stock will go down by that amount. A dividends increment causes a rise in the value of both calls and puts.

Strike Price

The strike price is a major component of any options contract. It also happens to be the sole static variable that affects an option's pricing. Each stock that can constitute an option has a different strike price and expiration date.

The strike price is typically determined using the stock's current market price. Take the example of a stock that is trading between $5 and $25. In this case, the strike price will vary with increments of about $2.50. The variations will be, for instance, $5, $10, $7.50, and so on. Let us assume that the stock price is trading between $25 and $200. In this instance, the strike price will progress in increments of $25, $35, $40, or basically in increments of $5.

A strike price of any option is among the most basic determinants of the specific option that you will pick for trading purposes. For instance, if IBM stock is trading at $550 and has a good chance of rising beyond $570 in the coming months. In this instance, you may consider purchasing a $600 call option that has an expiration date of at least two or even more months.

Now when holding this option, you will have the right to purchase IBM shares at $600 even as other purchases at prevailing market rates. This is because the option contract that you hold has effectively secured you the right to purchase at the said price.

Bid and Ask Price

Another crucial factor that plays an important part in option pricing is the bid or ask price. Each option, regardless of whether it is a call or put, always has a bid and ask price.

Basically, when buying options, you will purchase at the asking price or very close to it and sell on the bid or very near to it. For instance, if you are looking at September 75 calls and notice prices like $9.60 x $9.90 then the asking price, you'd be purchasing at is $9.90 while the selling price on this option has its lower margins at $9.60. The difference between these two prices is that the asking price and bid price is known as the spread. If the spread is very tight, then it means that the stock is very liquid.

Probability

The chance that an option will end up in the money is the main aspect influencing an option's worth. The closer the probability that the underlying asset will end up in the money gets to 100%, the greater the worth of the option becomes; the further away the probability that the underlying asset will finish in the money gets from 100%, the lower the value of the option. As a trader, you have to sharpen your analytical skills and determine whether an option is worthy of the premium it demands.

Stock Price

If you want to acquire an option that entitles you to buy a stock at $50 per share, the premium would be affected by how close the stock price is to the $50, i.e., you would pay more if the stock was trading at $45 as opposed to $40. The higher the stock price, the higher the premium of call options. In the same vein, the lower the stock price, the higher the premium of put options. If you want to sell an underlying at $30, you will pay more for the put option when the strike is at $28 as opposed to $35.

Time to Expiration

When there's a lot of time left for the options contract to expire, chances are high that the price of the underlying asset will undergo significant changes. Thus, the premium will be high. On the other hand, as the expiration approaches, the chances of significant change in the price of underlying assets tend to diminish, thus lowering the premium. The date of expiration causes options to have a definitive nature. Thus, if the price of an option seems unbearable, you might consider waiting for the period of expiration to come.

Natural Logarithm

The Black-Scholes calculation of premiums utilizes the natural logarithm. The changes in the price of underlying assets are proportional to the price of the underlying.

Normal Distribution

The normal probability distribution is used in the calculation of an options price. In the Black-Scholes model, price movement is understood to be distributed normally. Small movements have a high probability, whereas large movements have low probability.

News

It seems that financial news plays a critical role in driving the whole derivatives markets. Although chances of it happening are rare, influential finance journalists could drive an agenda that could trigger oscillations in the price of options contracts. However, the real captains of the industry are the brokers and market makers. These people who are in charge of brokerages and market-making corporations have the power to influence the course of the derivatives market. When they appear on the news, traders and investors hang on their every word and traders could go on a spree of buying or selling, which affects the value of options.

Crowd Psychology

If there's a sector that asks for mental maturity and discipline, it's the derivatives market. You have to have a plan and know when to take action as opposed to guessing your way around. But people are still people. It's so easy to get distracted by the trends and lose sight of your trading strategy. For instance, if a certain clique of traders reaps sudden profits, everyone runs into their niche in the hope of reaping quick benefits, thus driving the premium of the option up.

Price of the Underlying Asset

While they often will not move at the same speed or for the same amounts, an option is always going to follow the lead of its underlying asset. As such, you can always expect the price of related calls to increase along with rising asset prices, while puts will always decrease and vice versa.

Intrinsic Value

The amount of value that an option will hold onto, even at the very end of its lifespan, is known as the intrinsic value. When working with a call option you can find the intrinsic value by taking the current price of the underlying asset and dividing that by the difference between the strike price and the current price. When it comes to finding the intrinsic value of a put option, the process is mostly the same; to start, you subtract the amount the underlying asset is currently worth from its strike price before dividing that number by the current stock price.

The results of this equation will provide you with a clearer idea of the type of advantage that choosing to exercise the option at the moment would provide you with. This number can also be thought of as the minimum that the option will ever be worth, even at the moment of its expiration.

Calculating Intrinsic Value

To obtain the intrinsic value of a call option, you will simply deduct the call option's strike price from the stock's actual price or its prevailing market price.

Call Option Intrinsic Value = Stock (share) Price – Call Option Strike Price

An example:

Let us say that company ABC's stock is trading at $450, and its October $400 call option is asking for $50. The intrinsic value, in this case, is calculated by subtracting the call option strike price from the prevailing market price.

$450 - $400 = $50.

In our case above, the intrinsic value of the call option is $50. If this value it is negative, it simply means that the call option has no intrinsic value, and a put option has no extrinsic value.

Extrinsic Value

Extrinsic value can also be defined as the premium or time value of a put option. It is the part of the price that is determined by all other factors except for the value of the stock. The extrinsic value is the payment that you are making to the option seller to compensate for the risk that he or she takes for trading the options contract.

The money you are paying the trader or seller is referred to as risk money. The amount paid to the seller is considered justified and is essentially determined by several factors. These factors include dividends payable, volatility, interest rates, and expiration dates.

You will need a pricing model such as the Black-Scholes model if you wish to determine accurately the extrinsic value of any stock option, especially a put option. A stock's price is made up only of its extrinsic value if there is no intrinsic value built into it.

Chapter 7. Basic Option Strategies

The next thing we need to look at is some of the different strategies you can use when you want to trade-in options. Everyone needs to enter the market with some good strategies ahead of time. This makes it easier for them to make sure they enter the market at the right times, and that they can also pick the right times to exit the market.

The Long Call

This is a strategy that bets the asset will rise above the strike price before the expiration date. If you look at the underlying asset and the market and you think the price will rise before the options contract ends, then the long call is a good one to use.

If you do this call well, then the upside on this call can provide you with an infinite number of profits until the expiration, as long as that asset sees an increase in the price. Even if you see that the stock is moving in the wrong way, it is possible to salvage at least part of the premium you have by selling the call before it expires. The downside is a complete loss of the premium paid if the stock does not go up or starts to go down, but this is less risky than purchasing it outright.

The Long Put

The long put will be worth the most when you see the stock reaches $0 per share, so the maximal value will be the strike price multiplied 100 times the number of contracts you decide to do. You also benefit that if the asset price goes up, you can still sell the put and then save up some of the premium, as long as you still have a bit of time before your expiration. The most you can lose is all the loss of your premium based on how much you spend.

We want to use this one because the long put is a good way to wager on the asset declining. If you can stomach that you may potentially lose the whole premium, you can do this one. If you see a big decline in that asset, you will earn more with the puts than you would by short selling that stock.

The Short Put

The short put is seen as the opposite of the long put. The investor will sell their put, or they will go short. With this one, the investor is betting that the stock will stay flat or continue to rise until it reaches the expiration date. Remember that with this one, the other person is betting the price will go down and you hope it doesn't.

While a long call will bet that there will be a big increase in the value of a stock or other asset, the short put will be more modest and can pay off more modestly, though it can work in some situations.

Covered Calls

Another thing that we want to look at is the covered call. This is a good strategy because it will help reduce your risks of being alone on a long-term stock while making sure you can get some income in the process.

The trade-off that we will get with this one is that you need to be willing to sell off the shares you have at a set price, which will be the short strike price. Not sticking with this will cause you to lose money in the process. To help you execute this one, you need to purchase the underlying stock on the options contract, just like we talked about before. At the same time, we need to write or sell one of the call options on that same share.

Married Put

We can then move on to the second type of strategy that we can use within our options, and this one is known as the married put. In this strategy, the investor will purchase an asset, such as shares of a chosen stock. At the same time, they will purchase the put options for the same number of shares in that same stock.

The holder of the put option will then have the right to sell, within the time limits of the option, to sell the stock using that strike price, no matter what the stock's value is all about.

The reason that you, as an investor, would use this one is that it can help to protect them against any downside risk when they hold onto the stock. This strategy will then work just like an insurance policy and help establish the price floor if the price of the stock decides that it wants to turn and fall quickly.

Bull Call Spread

Now we can move on to a great strategy to learn about because it works well with options and in the stock market if you decide to purchase the stocks outright. With this strategy, known as the bull call spread, the investor will buy calls of an asset at a specific strike price, and then at the same time they will buy the same number of calls, but at a strike price that is higher. Both of these will come with the same asset, so don't try to do it with two different ones, and they will have the same expiration with them.

Bear Put Spread

We spent some time talking about the bull call spread and how to use it when we think the market is bullish. However, there are times when the market will go in the opposite direction, and we will end up with a bearish market instead. This is why working with a bear put spread could be the best option to help you out here.

Protective Collar

Sometimes it is a good idea to find ways to protect yourself in the market. It would be nice if the stock market, or any other underlying asset that you use with options, would follow a pattern that made sense and always stayed the same. But if that happened, then everyone would get into the market, and you would not be able to make the money you want. The good news is that the protective collar strategy will help you get this done, ensuring you are protected in the market.

The Long Straddle

You can't look much at the world of investing without looking at some of the straddle options out there. This is a great strategy that you can use to provide you with lots of choices and make it easier for you to stay protected and make as much money as possible. We will spend some time looking at how to complete what is known as a long straddle. The long straddle strategy will be one where the investor can purchase the put and the call option simultaneously. You want to do this with the same asset underneath the option, with the same strike price and expiration date. Everything has to be the same on this one, except that you do one put option and one call option.

The Long Strangle

In the long strangle strategy, the investor will spend their time working on an out of the money call option, while also going through and doing an out of the money put option at the same time. We need to make sure the underlying asset of both is the same and that we keep the expiration date the same. This can help you to protect yourself if you are not certain which direction the market will go.

Long Call Butterfly Spread

This is a fun one that allows you to stay in the market a bit longer and can make it easier for you to see some results with what you are doing here. However, we have to make sure that we use it well and get in and out at the right parts along the way. The strategy we will talk about here is known as a long call butterfly spread. All of the other strategies we have looked at so far in this guidebook were a combination of two contracts or two positions. With this one, though, we will want to use the call options. With this one, the investor will combine both the bear spread, and the bull spread strategies explained earlier in this guidebook. You would also need to make sure you work with three strike prices that are different. You will still stick with the same expiration date and the same underlying assets along the way to make this happen.

Iron Condor

The next option that we are going to add to our list is known as the iron condor. This one is really interesting and allows us to work on many different things at once to see some results. The way to construct the iron condor is to sell one of your out of the money puts, and then we go through the process of selling one out of the money call while also buying one out of the money call, making sure we do this last one at a higher strike price.

Iron Butterfly Strategy

Then it is time to move on to a strategy that is known as the iron butterfly strategy. We talked about the iron condor and the butterfly spread, so now we get to have some fun and work with the iron butterfly strategy. To make this one work, the investor will need to sell one of them at the money puts, and then they can buy an out of the money put, while also taking the time to sell one of them at the money calls and purchasing an out of the money call. This is a lot of steps, so make sure you know the market and how it is supposed to work before you start.

Chapter 8. Day Trading and Swing Trading

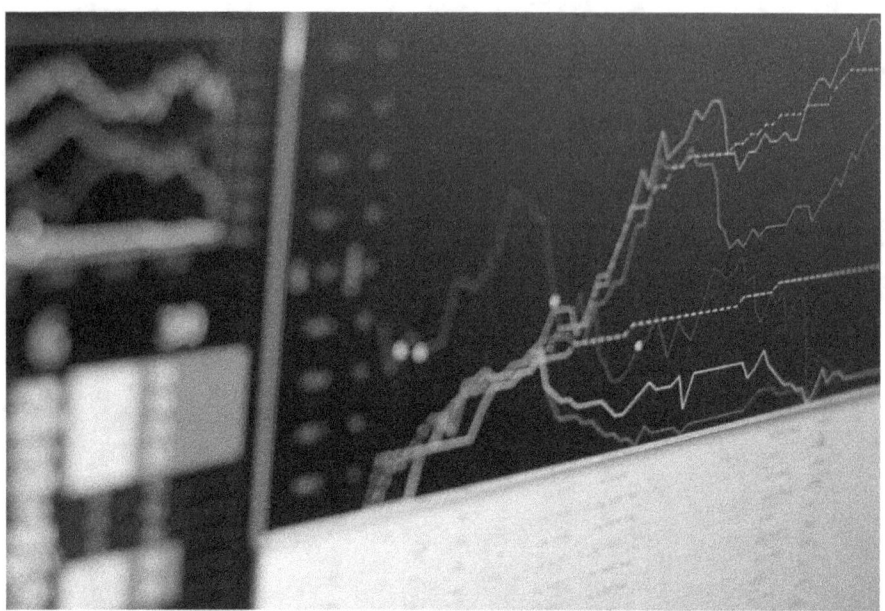

A basic question to start with is this one—what are you looking for like a day trader? The answer here is quite easy.

First, you must look for stocks that are following a predictable trend. Then, you need to trade them in one single day. You don't need to keep them longer than a day.

If you purchase stocks of Amazon (AMZN) today, you should not hold the stocks overnight and sell them tomorrow. It is no longer day trading if you hold on to your position. That one is called swing trading.

As a day trader, you need to understand the difference between day trading and swing trading. The latter is a type of trading in which you hold the stocks over a certain period, usually from one day to several weeks. This is a different trading style, and you must not use these tools and strategies that are ideal for day trading if you want to follow the swing trading style.

Remember, day trading is a business (Rule 2). Swing trading is also a business, albeit a different type of business. The differences between day trading and swing trading are similar to the differences between owning a meat processing plant and a hamburger chain.

Both businesses involve food, but these are not similar. They operate with different revenue models, market segments, regulations, and time frames. You must not confuse day trading with other trading styles because the trades are performed in the stock market.

Professional day traders close their positions before the stock market closes. Many traders perform both swing trading and day trading. They are aware that they are running two different businesses, and they are trained to manage the risks of these two types of trading.

One of the main differences between swing trading and day trading is the style of choosing stocks. Many traders do not day trade and swing trade the same stocks. Swing traders often look for stocks in established companies that they know will not lose their value in a few weeks.

However, for day trading, you can trade any stock you want including companies that are predicted to go bankrupt. Day traders don't care what happens to the stocks after the market closes.

Many of the companies you Day Trade are quite risky to hold overnight because they may lose much of their value quickly.

Before you begin to trade, you need to determine how active you want to be. You need to ask yourself questions like: how much time do I have at hand, and what are my current responsibilities?

Your answers to these questions will help you to decide if you want to trade daily or if you want to buy and hold for some days or weeks.

There are two groups of active traders: the day traders and the swing traders. Both groups have a similar goal of making profits from short-term or long-term trades. However, there are major differences between the two that you should understand and decide on your best choice depending on your level of technical expertise, time frames, and preference.

Day trading is a form of trading where your long or short position is entered and exited on the same day—opens and closes within 24hours. Day traders get into positions based on quantitative, fundamental, or technical reasons. Day traders do not hold their positions overnight. On the other hand, Swing trading is a long-term investment where the trader buys or shorts securities and holds them for some days, weeks, or months. Unlike day traders, the swing traders do not intend to take trading as a full-time job.

You do not need to have lots of capital to swing trade, while day trading follows the 'pattern day trader rule.'

This rule governs any trader that makes more than four trades in the same security over five business days. This trader is referred to as a "pattern day trader" based on the premise that the trades represent above 6% of the trader's total trading activity in that period. A pattern day trader must also have a minimum of $25,000 equity in their account on any trading day.

Day Trading

However, being a day trader can be very beneficial; it has its inherent risks. A day trader needs to realize that there may be times where he may encounter a 100% loss.

More than some other type of trading, Day trading requires quick and right choices on positions and estimating the entry, exits, and stop-losses. The trades are fast and must be amazingly precise. Day trading imperatively requires being available and comprehending whatever occurs in the market at every point in time. Even though it doesn't imply that one should trade every day or consistently, the evaluations need to be done frequently. This type of trading takes more time than swing trading. However, it can be satisfying all-day work.

Day trading is better for people who have a passion for full-time trading and possess discipline, decisiveness, and diligence. To be successful as a day trader, he needs to have an in-depth understanding of charts and technical trading. Day trading can be stressful and intense, and so, traders need to be able to control their emotions and stay calm under fire.

Swing Trading

A swing trader identifies swings in currencies, commodities, and stocks that occur over days. Unlike day trading, a swing trade may take up to weeks to work out. Swing traders have more persistence concerning their trade opening. As the positions extend to the second day, there is potential for huge benefits on a single trade, yet there are fewer trading opens generally. Anyone who has the investment capital and knowledge can give a shot at swing trading.

Swing trading requires less technical investigative abilities and progressively focus research and information on macroeconomics. The entry focus does not need to be that exact, and the planning isn't so pivotal since the moves, which swing traders are expecting to get are bigger.

Swing trading does not require the trader to spend a lot of time, as there is no need for frequent technical evaluations and constantly sitting in front of the screen. It is usually a stress-free and low-effort job. The swing trader can have a separate full-time job as he does not have to stay glued to his computer screen all day.

Swing traders usually require time to work out. The more time a trade is open for days or weeks, the more the chances of having higher profits than trading multiple times daily on the same security. Margin requirements in a swing trade are higher since positions are held overnight. Compared to day trading whose maximum leverage is four times one's capital, swing trading is often two times the trader's capital.

Be that trader who needs to understand and utilize stop-losses and target levels to their benefit. While there is the possibility that the stop order will execute at an unfavorable price, it is still better than having to monitor all your open positions constantly.

As is normal with all types of trading, a swing trader can also experience losses, and because the traders hold the positions for a longer time, they may experience greater loss than the day traders.

Swing trading does not require the use of state-of-the-art technology. You can swing trade with one computer, and any needed trading tools.

Because swing trading is usually not a full-time job, the traders have other income sources and have reduced chances of burnout caused by stress.

When Should You Go for Day Trading?

The points below have summarized the ideal situation for you to be a day trader:

- You are disciplined, diligent, and strong-willed.

- You are willing to make small profits daily by making small trades.

- You have the minimum capital requirements stated by FINRA rules for pattern day traders and SEC, if and when they apply to you.

- You are knowledgeable and have the expertise to make great profits.

- You are not easily stressed, and you can manage stress.

- You are committed to studying current trends and can take needed action at the speed of light.

- You never have a dull day, and you are out for excitement every minute.

When Should You Go for Swing Trading?

The points below have summarized the ideal situation for you to be a swing trader:

- You lack extreme levels of technical understanding.

- You do not want to go full time into trading. That is, you don't desire trading as your only source of income.

- You do not like stress and will instead go for something that is not as risky as day trading.

- You do not fancy constant monitoring of market activities.

- You are patient and can wait for weeks to months while studying the movements of the market.

- You have a full-time job and can't spare time for day trading activities.

- You do not have plenty of money to invest.

Chapter 9. Mistakes to Avoid in Option Trading

Options trading is every trader's point of interest, and you can make handsome profits from it too. If you have come this far in the book, you already know the potential that this field has, but it can be equally devastating for your career if you make the wrong trades. So, if you want to take this seriously, here are some mistakes that are commonly made, and once you know them beforehand, you will think twice before making them yourselves.

Not Having a Trading Plan

Not following any trading plan is probably the most common mistake of all, especially among beginners. It might be that you read in some finance magazine that a particular company's stocks are performing well, or maybe you got a tip at a random gathering, and you decided to act it. Well, should you? The answer is both yes and no. No, because you should never take anyone on their word when it comes to trading. Yes, because it might turn out to be a good tip in certain cases, but you first have to perform a bit of research of your own and then decide whether that tip is worth believing in or not.

If you do not have a trading plan before diving into the world of options trading, it is simply as if you are driving your car, and you do not have a license. So, when you face a crisis situation, the losses can be huge. In options, you do not have all the time in the world. There is a fixed amount of time within which you have to take action; otherwise, your option will expire worthlessly. You always have to be alert for any opportunities that might come your way and if there is an opportunity, don't ever miss it. So, your goal of making a lot of money might not just be in your favor just because you did not plan for it. Remember that no matter how good your strategy is, sometimes they can fail when you do not have a trading plan.

Some of the things that your trading plan should possess are the type of options that you are particularly interested in like Nifty, Equity, Commodities, and so on. The amount of money that you can afford to invest in trading every month, the amount of money you want to invest in each trade, your risk appetite, and your expected return from a trade. Make sure that this plan is followed for every trade that you conduct. You will be tempted to go off the track, but you have to resist those temptations and prevent yourself from risking too much. Your fear and greed both have to be controlled if you want to make it big. If you are just a beginner, start small and then work your way up to the top slowly and steadily.

Believing in the One-Size-Fits-All Concept

Selecting the strategy that would work best for you, depending on the market's situation is what options trading is all about. Suppose you figured out a good strategy, and you have been using it for quite some time, and it is working out well for you. However, that specific strategy is not meant for all types of trades. For example, you cannot use strategies of a bullish market in a bearish one. So, if you keep repeating your strategy without ever evaluating the trades, thinking that it will work like some magic wand and make you win every trade, then you are wrong. You have to learn to predict the market outlook and then choose the best strategy for you.

You have to perform technical analysis and fundamental analysis to find out which strategies you should use. Both macro and microeconomic factors have to be taken into consideration. Gather knowledge from different places by reading books and going to workshops. Read the views of experts from different reputed finance magazines. After you have figured out the market outlook, picking the right strategy would become much easier.

You have already read about the book's important strategies, and you know when you have to apply each of them.

Ignoring the Expiration Date

The expiration date of options is one of the major factors affecting our trades. As you know, to make profits you have to speculate on the direction of the stock movement. At the same time, I am also asking you to speculate how much time it is going to take a particular point because, in the case of options where your time is limited by expiration date, it cannot take you forever. Let us say that you researched and found some factors that can positively impact the stock price, but do you know when that price is going to reach the level you want it to reach?

Trading does not only mean looking after strategies. In the case of options, you have to look out for the expiration dates as well. Like the strategies, when it comes to the expiration date, you have many choices for it. You should keep in your checklist some questions because then it becomes easier to figure it out. For example, you can ask yourself how much time you think a particular trade will need to play out. You can also ask yourself whether you want to hold a trade through major events or not like a stock split or a public announcement. Lastly, you should also ask yourself whether you have the required liquidity to pursue after this.

Overleveraging the Trades

It is always advised to beginners to get used to stock investment before you start options trading. When you have done stocks investing first, it is more likely for you to have handled huge amounts of money directly, and in fact, buying stocks directly also means that you have to pay the entire share price.

For this example, let us say that you are a person who can buy stocks worth $1000 at a time, and let's say that you have done this before but not in options. Now you have switched over to the options because of their affordable nature because they are a derivative. If you had to buy the underlying asset directly with all your money, it would have cost you way more money than what you're investing in purchasing the options. Therefore, you don't need to invest a thousand dollars for purchasing that many amounts of stocks in the form of options contracts.

But this also poses a risk—a risk where you might end up overleveraging. Leverage is a powerful tool only when you use it wisely. Just because there is leverage, doesn't mean that you should invest a bigger amount than necessary.

That is why there is a very common rule that is followed—consider it as a rule of thumb in your case. Try and limit your loss to within 5% for every trade that you do. You must strictly comply with this so that not all your capital is lost behind a particular trade. When you lose only some money in a trade, you can always pick yourself back up and invest in a different trade, which brings me to the next point.

Error in Position Sizing of Your Trades

Two common emotions are responsible for all errors related to position sizing. These emotions are greed and fear. Suppose you are making a decision, and you become too greedy about your profits, you might position your trade too big so that it is not right for the size of your account. And this is even more common when your outlook of the market is wrong and then what you get in return is not profit but a crippling loss, recovering from it can become difficult.

This was just one mistake of position sizing. The other one is when you position your trade too small. There is nothing wrong with trading small, but do you know what it means? It means that you might not get the chance to make any substantial profit at all.

Here are some common ways in which you can maintain appropriate position sizing:

- Ensure the risk percentage for each trade is somewhere around 1-5% of your total account value.

- It is better for every trade that you stick to a consistent dollar value like $100 or $1000 based on how much you can afford to risk.

No matter what you do or which strategy you use, your position sizing should be such that you are comfortable risking that amount of money. In simpler terms, even if the trade does not happen like you predicted it to be, it won't hurt you to lose the money invested. In the ideal case, your trade value should be such that it is meaningful enough, but not too big that it has reason to make you lose your sleep at night.

Buying Options Based on Whether They Are Cheap or Not

Human beings tend to think that it is better to buy it whenever something is cheap rather than going for something costly. They think that this is the most cost-effective thing to do. However, what you don't understand is that following this 'cheap' tactic is not going to help you with options. It is going to ruin your trade. It is usually said that an option tends to be more out-of-the-money when its premium is more towards the lower side. Yes, at first glance, it might appear to you that you have just found the biggest steal of your life but trust me when I say this, don't fall for the trap because even if you get it, making any money with the help of that option would be highly unlikely.

When the premiums of options are towards the lower side, those options' strike price is usually either well below or well above the market price. In simpler words, if you had to make money with such an option, then there has to be a miraculous change in the price for you to do so. So, let us say you bought a call option with a very low premium, and if you want to make money with it, it has to show a drastic movement upward. Similarly, there has to be a drastic movement downward if you want to make money after buying a put option with a low premium.

Chapter 10. Successful Trading During the First 30 Minutes

The first hour of the trading day tends to be the most profitable and how can you take advantage of that trend? In addition, we will be looking at some of the best strategies, which you can implement when considering your first few trades of the day.

As with your regular day-to-day life, the first hour is the most crucial. If you have a good first hour, or the first few minutes at the beginning of your day, you can set yourself up to be successful for the rest of the day. With day trading, the same concept applies.

If you establish a successful routine as soon as the day gets started, you will be able to make some very good profits early on. That can set the tone for a successful trading day. So, it certainly pays to set things up for a positive vibe throughout the day.

It is worth taking this into account when crafting your opening hour strategy. The more you can plan ahead for that first hour of the day, the more you can profit from trends carrying over into the new trading day.

In addition, making the most of the first trading hour makes sense, as this is when most day traders are looking to place their bets for the day. This is important to note, as not all day traders are full-time day traders. So, they will look to place their trades early on in hopes of setting their positions for the rest of the day.

If you happen to be a full-time day trader, then you will certainly have a leg up on your fellow traders. Even if you aren't a full-time day trader, but have access to your computer throughout your day, then you can certainly make key trades at various parts of the day. Most importantly, you can avoid certain hours in the day.

Why Trade in the First Hour?

The numbers show that the first hour of the day is when most of the action happens. Roughly, 20% of all trends happen for the rest of the day.

What does that mean?

It means that the greatest amount of movement and volatility happens at the beginning of the day, and that is great news for day traders.

Now, the casual day trader won't be fully positioned to appreciate the first hour. As I mentioned earlier, they will most likely place their trades early, perhaps set up options or other positions, and wait for the day to unfold.

While this isn't a bad strategy, it is not one that will maximize your returns. If anything, you might find yourself missing out on some potential gains simply because you did not take full advantage of that first hour.

Now, the reason why the first hour is so important is due to the volume of trading that goes on during that first hour. In fact, the volume and liquidity that swirls around that first hour are such that you can make trades and profits within minutes.

This is important to note, as most of the trade tends to settle down throughout the day.

When you are looking to trade during the rest of the day, the other time where it does get fast and furious is right at the end of the day. This is another time in which you can make some profits.

As such, the morning is all about liquidity coming and going; that is, everyone is placing their trades and waiting for the rest of the day unfold. The end of the day is everyone trying to liquidate their positions before the close of the day, or at least trying to set themselves up for the next day.

It should also be noted that for you to make real headway in trading during the first hour, you would need to have some cash at your disposal and stocks with a high trade volume.

Bear in mind that success in the first hour is all about volume, that is, stocks that have a degree of volume means that they are being traded frequently. This is important, as you will make money of value and not so much on the actual value of the stock.

Think about this example:

You bought stock in ABC company right at the beginning of the day. If this stock has low volume, say it is traded roughly every half hour, then you would only have one chance, two at most, to make money during the first hour.

So, let's assume that you got the stock at $10 a share. If you trade 100 shares, that's $1,000 worth of stock. Now, you sell at $10.50. That is a sale of $1,050. In short, you make $50 on the trade. If you do that twice in the first hour, that is a profit of $100 in that first hour.

That would be a 10% return on the initial $1,000. While that's not bad, you could do better.

Now, let's assume you have found four stocks in a similar range. If you pulled off the exact same trade four times in that first hour, you would be making $200 instead of $100. If you could make six trades, that would give you $300 and so on.

The point of this example is that you can make a far larger amount of money by executing more trades, even if the yield is lower than hoping to make one huge trade. As you can see, the key is with the number. The more successful trades you make, the more money you will make.

You could further compound your profits if you were working with a higher share volume. But, what about if you made similar trades on the base of 1,000 shares? What about 10,000 shares? I hope you see where I am going with this.

However, most day traders don't start off with massive capital. So, they need to work their way up. By using this approach, you can work your way up from $1,000 trades to larger trades as you gain momentum.

The First 5 Minutes

Believe it or not, the first 5 minutes are crucial to setting yourself up for success during your trading day. If you set things upright, you can certainly cash in on the momentum of the first few minutes.

Now, there is a simple explanation of why the first 5 minutes tend to be most fast and furious: the gaps.

Let's say that stock was climbing up in price, but got stuck as the trading day shut down. This is important to note because investors are going to want to pick up where they left off. This means that at the outset of the next trading day, there will be a spike in the price of that stock.

This is the gap.

Under this assumption, the closing price of a given stock was $5. At the outset of the next trading day, the price suddenly spiked to $7. Those that got in at $5 could stand to make a good profit if they manage to sell at $7.

In fact, "playing the gap" is one of the few reasons why I advocate for holding positions open overnight. This is highly speculative, but if you are riding a trend, you could make some considerable gains within the first few minutes of trading.

It should be noted that if you are looking to play the gap, then you need to sell very early on in the next trading day. The reason for this is that the pullback on the stock will be very hard to predict and will happen very quickly.

The pullback consists of the price of the stock reverting to its trend or close to it. Therefore, you could spot a double top or even a triple top pattern. However, if the stock's spike breaks its resistance level, you might consider purchasing more stock on the dip in order to anticipate another surge as part of a third spike either following the double top or perhaps as a breakout following the triple top.

This is why playing gaps can be an extreme sport thanks to the adrenaline rush you get from speculating in these first few minutes of the trading day. So, I would encourage you to play those gaps once you have gotten your feet wet as a day trader. Otherwise, taking advantage of the fast pace at the outset of the trading day can certainly help you set the tone for a positive trading day.

The Next Couple of Hours

Once the dust settles on the first hour of trading, the next couple of hours tend to be a lot less fast-paced. In fact, the volume of trading declines significantly. While there are still transactions going on, the least traded stocks and assets will almost grind to a halt while only the most highly traded assets will still register movement on the radar.

This is the time when you can get yourself a cup of coffee or perhaps take a break.

The reason for this sudden drop in volatility and movement is because most investors are looking to reload and set up their positions for the rest of the day. In fact, many of them would be looking to set up their positions for the end of the day.

Bear in mind that many developments take place throughout the business day. So, investors are generally on the lookout for announcements by the government concerning economic data or announcements from the Fed regarding meetings and decisions such as interest rate hikes or cuts.

Every week, the government is reporting numbers. So, investors are always looking to wait and see what happens with this data before committing their positions. Consequently, they will be keen to make sure that they don't commit too soon and either get burned or miss the boat.

Chapter 11. Tips for Success

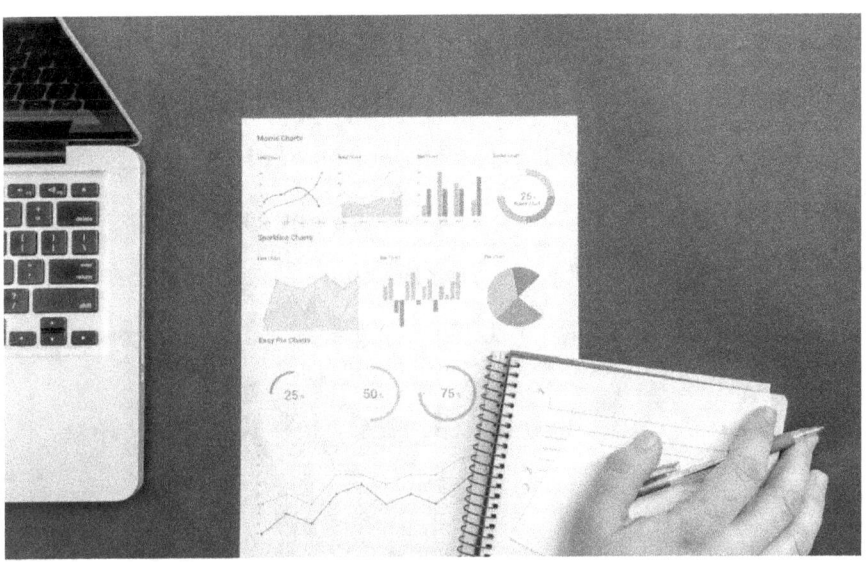

Know When to Improvise Your Plan

While having a plan in options trading is of utmost importance, it is essential to know when your project needs improvement. There will be times when you have to move away from your plan, even when your emotions tell you to stick to it. A successful trader knows when their goal is no longer valid for the current situation. Having a plan sets your path, but this does not mean that you will follow it blindly to the end of the world. Traders come to a point where something out of control happens, which renders their plan useless for that situation.

That is why, when you plan, know what its weak points are and when it can fail. The market conditions keep changing frequently, so what is true today might not be applicable tomorrow. So, if you are thinking of following your predetermined course of action even when the conditions of the market have taken a 360-degree turn, then you are making a big mistake. It will only lead you to your failure. Yes, it will require a lot of practice to understand your emotions, hold you back, and change situations. However, every small step in the right direction is progress, which includes being aware of the disparity.

Always Have Your Exit and Entry Plan Ready before Starting

When it comes to options trading, figuring out the right entries and exits is probably one thing you should learn well. No matter how good your adjustment techniques are, nothing can correct a wrong entry, and you might end up incurring huge losses because of that.

However, there is something else that is even more important than learning to set the correct entry and exit points. Can you guess what it is? Understanding that you have to exercise your entry and exit points before the money is off the table. New options traders have this idea that every trade has to fetch your vast profits, and you need every last cent out of it, but you have to break free from this mentality. It can pose a big hurdle for every new trader. As long as you have a trading plan that is solid and profitable, there will be several trades in the future that can fetch you profits. So, sticking to only one of them as if it is the last trade you will perform is wrong, and it will only end up giving you a loss.

So, stop worrying about those small extra profits because you have already made a certain amount of profit from the trade, and now you have to protect that. Yes, there is a chance that if you ignore this advice and continue with your trading mentality, you might make a few extra bucks here and there, but the odds are that the loss will be more than the gain. You will end up losing the profit you made without even getting the chance to pull the trigger.

Avoid Out-of-the-Money Trades

A few strategies can help you make a profit by buying out-of-the-money call options, but they are indeed the exception. You, as a new investor in options trading, might feel attracted to the out-of-the-money call options because they are affordable and cheap. Still, you need to remind yourself that the stock market and the options market are two different scenarios. Even if you look at the underlying stocks to buy the options, it is not viable to buy low and then sell high. In case a call has become out-of-the-money, then there is very little chance for it to rise to the required levels before it approaches its expiration date again. If you still buy these options, you are just a step away from gambling with your money.

Don't Shrink Your Homework

There are so many instances where options traders lose sides just because they did not perform their homework. If you ask the new traders, you will often find that they are guilty of not conducting extensive and adequate market research. They even fail to possess due diligence before making a trade. Do you know why I am stressing so much about performing your homework correctly? If you don't, you will never be aware of the timing of the data releases, the seasonal trends, or trading patterns, all of which are experienced traders. New traders are so overwhelmed with the idea of making a trade as soon as possible that they do not think it is ideal to do some research, and then this turns out to be quite an expensive lesson for them.

Even if you are not interested in an investment, you should still take some time out to research it. When you perform thorough research, you will get to know everything about a particular financial statement, and you will also be fully aware of the path you are treading. For example, if you decide to invest in options, you need to research the various strategies you can apply. Remember that every other trader has access to the same information as you, so you can even identify the investments that will provide good results if you give the effort.

You should also make a promise to yourself t that you will read at least one new book on options trading every week. When you read books, you learn many secrets, and you also know many new things. You will also acquire a more profound knowledge of the rewards and risks involved in options trading.

Don't Trade for Wealth but Income

If you think that options trading will give you returns like 150%, you need to take a step back and reconsider. Yes, there might indeed be certain investments once in a while that will give you such figures, but not every trade is like that. Most new traders think that options trading will make them wealthy overnight, but there is no such thing as that.

If you believe that you are doing options trading for wealth generation, you have got it all wrong. It is more like devising the right strategy to get a regular income. If you become hungry for more profits, you will be more likely to overlook the risky endeavors and invest your money anyway. Never forget that options trading can be full of risks, so you must take your steps carefully.

Never Believe in Unfounded Tips

Another prevalent mistake that new traders make is that they start believing in random tips. Almost every trader made this mistake at some point in their life. It might be that one of your friends or relatives has been going on discussing a specific company whose stocks are performing well, and maybe they are going to make a groundbreaking profit by investing in that stock. What you should do is do your research before believing anything. I am not saying whatever they are saying is false. It can be correct, but that does not mean you have to pounce on it right away as if it is the next big thing, and you are going to lose it if you do not go for it now. Take a step back before rushing to your online brokerage right now and do your research.

The example mentioned above is of only one source of unfounded tips. Another one comes from social media and television. You will often find investment professionals on the media who can't stop talking about a particular stock as it is a must investment. Still, if you probe into the matter deeply, you will find that it has nothing extraordinary about it. You have to remind yourself that if you keep following media tips, it is nothing more than a speculative gamble in the world of trading.

However, all this talk about unfounded tips does not mean you should turn a blind eye to every information you receive. If there is something that has caught your attention and you can't let go of it, then your first task would be to think whether the source is reliable or not. The next step is performing your homework, and this will give you the information you need. So, don't rely on anyone telling you what to do. You need to figure out whether or not that will be the right type of investment for you. You can also look for a second opinion from someone reliable and unbiased.

Start with Enough Capital

Although you do not need much capital to start, it is also true that you should have enough capital to get you set up. In simpler terms, wealth is the amount of money you should keep in your trading account to clear any money required for the transactions, and this same capital will help you if you incur a loss during trading.

Your trading account should always have some amount of money on it. When you are making trades, you should not worry about funds transfer, and the money already being present in your account means things will work out smoothly. Your broker can also help you out without any delay from fund transfer. If you ask the successful traders in the market, all of them will say the same thing. They always keep some money in their account and keep checking their balance from time to time so that even if they have a few unfavorable trades in the future, the money in the report will act as a cushion for them.

Don't Purchase Too Much with Margin

'Margin' was explained at the beginning of this book. It is when you purchase options by borrowing some money from your broker. In some cases, you can make more money with the help of margins, but on the contrary, if you face losses, they will become even more exaggerated because of the margins. So, you need to have a proper understanding of how margin works. You also need to understand that using margins also means your broker can ask you any time to sell your options.

New traders often get carried away because they think margins mean free money, so they keep using it until the nightmare comes. For example, suppose you have used margin, but then the investment turned worse.

It means you have a considerable debt obligation to the broker for nothing because you did not get any profits at all. It is somewhat similar to buying options with your credit card. Would you do that? No, right? It is the same thing when you use margins excessively.

Chapter 12. Market Trends

A market is a chaotic place, with several traders vying for dominance over one another. There is countless number of strategies and time frames in play, and at any point, it is close to impossible to determine who will emerge with the upper hand. In such an environment, how is it then possible to make any money? After all, if everything is unpredictable, how can you get your picks, right?

Well, this is where thinking in terms of probabilities comes into play. While you cannot get every single bet right, as long as you get enough right and make enough money on those to offset your losses, you will make money in the long run.

It's not about getting one or two right. It's about executing the strategy with the best odds of winning over and over again, and ensuring that your math works out with regards to the relationship between your win rate and average win.

So, it comes down to finding patterns, which repeat themselves over time in the markets. What causes these patterns? Well, the other traders, of course! To put it more accurately, the orders that the other traders place in the market are what create patterns that repeat themselves over time.

The first step to understanding these patterns is to understand what trends and ranges are. Identifying them and learning to spot when they transition into one another will give you a massive leg up not only with your options trading but also with directional trading.

Trends

In theory, spotting a trend is simple enough. Look left to right, and if the price is headed up or down, it's a trend. Well, sometimes it is that simple. However, for the majority of the time, you have both with and counter-trend forces operating in the market. It is possible to have a long counter-trend reaction within a larger trend, and sometimes, depending on the time frame you're in, these counter-trend reactions take up the majority of your screen space.

Trend vs. Range

This is a chart of the UK100 CFD, which mimics the FTSE 100, on the four-hour time frame. Three-quarters of the chart is a downtrend, and the last quarter is a wild uptrend. Using the looking left to the right guideline; we'd conclude that this instrument is in a range. Is that true, though?

Just looking at that chart, you can see that short-term momentum is bullish. So, if you were considering taking a trade on this, would you implement a range strategy or a trending one? This is exactly the sort of thing that catches traders up.

The key to deciphering trends is to watch for two things: counter-trend participation quality and turning points. Let's tackle counter-trend participation first.

Counter-Trend Participation

When a new trend begins, the market experiences an extremely imbalanced order flow, which is tilted towards one side. There's not much counter-trend participation against this seeming tidal wave of trend orders. Price marches on without any opposition and experiences only a few hiccups.

As time goes on, though, the trend forces run out of steam and have to take breaks to gather themselves. This is where counter-trend traders start testing the trend and trying to see how far back into the trend they can go. While it is unrealistic to expect a full reversal at this point, the quality of the correction or pushback tells us a lot about the strength distribution between the with and counter-trend forces.

While all this is going on behind the scenes, the price chart is what records the push and pull between these two forces. Using the price chart, we cannot only anticipate when a trend is coming to an end, but also how long it could potentially take before it does. This second factor, which helps us estimate the time it could take, is invaluable from an options perspective, especially if you're using a horizontal spread strategy.

In all cases, the greater the number of them, the greater the counter-trend participation in the market. The closer a trend is to end, the greater the counter-trend participation. Thus, the minute you begin to see price move into a large, sideways move with an equal number of buyers and sellers in it, you can be sure that some form of redistribution is going on.

Mind you, and the trend might continue or reverse. Either way, it doesn't matter. What matters is that you know the trend is weak and that now is probably not the time to be banking on-trend strategies.

Starting from the left, we can see that there is close to no counter-trend bars, bearish in this case, and the bulls make easy progress. Note the angle with which the bulls proceed upwards.

Then comes the first major correction, and the counter-trend players push back against the last third of the bull move. Notice how strong the bearish bars are and note their characters compared to the bullish bars.

The bulls recover and push the price higher at the original angle and without any bearish presence, which seems odd. This is soon explained as the bears' slam price back down, and for a while, it looks as if they've managed to form a V top reversal in the trend, which is an extremely rare occurrence.

The price action that follows is a more accurate reflection of the power in the market, with both bulls and bears sharing chunks of the order flow, with overall order flow in the bull's favor but only just. Price here is certainly in an uptrend, but looking at the extent of the bearish pushbacks, perhaps we should be on our guard for a bearish reversal. After all, the order flow is looking pretty sideways at this point.

So how would we approach an options strategy with the chart in the state it is in at the extreme, right? Well, for one, any strategy that requires an option beyond the near month is out of the question, given the probability of it turning. Secondly, looking at the order flow it does seem to be following a channel, doesn't it?

While the channel isn't very clean if you were aggressive enough, you could consider deploying a collar with the strike prices above and below this channel to take advantage of the price movement. You could also employ some moderately bullish strategies as price approaches the bottom of this channel and figuring out the extent of the bull move is easier thanks to you being able to reference the top of the channel.

As price moves in this channel, it's all well and good. Eventually, though, we know that the trend has to flip. How do we know when this happens?

Turning Points

As bulls and bears struggle over who gets to control the order flow, price swings up and down. You will notice that every time price comes back into the 6427-6349 zone, the bulls seem to step in masse and repulse the bears.

This tells us that the bulls are willing to defend this level in large numbers and strongly at that. Given the number of times the bears have tested this level, we can safely assume that above this level, bullish strength is a bit weak. However, at this level, it is as if the bulls have retreated and are treating this as a sort of last resort, for the trend to be maintained. You can see where I'm going with this.

If this level were to be breached by the bears, it is a good bet that a large number of bulls will be taken out. In martial terms, the largest army of bulls has been marshaled at this level. If this force is defeated, it is unlikely that there's going to be too much resistance to the bears below this level.

This zone, in short, is a turning point. If price breaches this zone decisively, we can safely assume that the bears have moved in and control the majority of the order flow.

Turning Point Breached

The two horizontal lines mark the decisive turning point zone, and the price touches this level twice more and is repulsed by the bulls. Notice how the last bounce before the level breaks produces an extremely weak bullish bounce, and price simply caves through this. Notice the strength with which the bears breakthrough.

For now, we can conclude that as long as the price remains below the turning point, we are bearishly biased. You can see this by looking at the angle with which bulls push back as well as the lack of strong bearish participation on the push upwards.

This doesn't mean we go ahead and pencil in a bull move and start implementing strategies that take advantage of the upcoming bullish move. Remember, nothing is for certain in the markets. Don't change your bias or strategy until the turning point decisively breaks.

Some key things to note here are that a turning point is always a major S/R level. It is usually a swing point where a large number of trend forces gather to support the trend. This will not always be the case, so don't make the mistake of hanging on to older turning points.

This indicates that the bears are quite strong here and that any subsequent attack will be handled the same way until the level breaks. Do we know when the level will break? Well, we can't say with any accuracy. However, we can estimate the probability of it breaking.

The latest upswing has seen very little bearish pushback, comparatively speaking, and the push into the level is strong. Instinct would say that there's one more rejection left here. However, who knows? Until the level breaks, we stay bearish. When the level breaks, we switch to the bullish side.

Putting It All Together

So now we're ready to put all of this together into one coherent package. Your analysis should always begin with determining the current state of the market. Ranges are pretty straightforward to spot, and they occur either within big pullbacks in trends or at the end of trends.

Trends vary in strength, depending on the amount of counter-trend participation they have. The way to determine counter-trend participation levels is to simply look at the price bars and compare the counter-trend ones to the trendy ones. The angle with which the trend progresses is a great gauge as well, for its strength, with steeper angles being stronger.

Chapter 13. Why Trade Options?

It's useful to know why we are trading options in the first place. The fact that they are cheap is only one factor to consider. Knowing what they are is going to help you make the right investment decisions.

Options Provide Leverage

When you buy an options contract, you control 100 shares of stock for that option's lifetime. The option is a tool that allows you to control those shares of stock without paying the full price for them. For example, Apple may be trading at $200 a share. An options contract on Apple might cost $125 for a particular strike price. If I had purchased the shares, the cost would be $200/share x 100 shares = $20,000. So, for 0.625% of the shares' price, either I can control the shares for the time until the options contract expires or I sell it.

Options Are Inexpensive

OK, this is a restatement of the point above, but to buy shares you need a lot of money. Yes, you could buy one share of Apple, but if Apple's price goes up to $1, what you've made is $1. To profit using stock shares, say by swing trading, you need to own a lot of stock shares. As we'll see in a minute price changes in the stock are magnified in the option. If Apple goes up to $1, the options trader will be a lot better off than the guy who only buys one share with his $200.

Options Prices Change in Big Ways

However, the price or value of an option is directly related to the share price of the stock. It's not a one-to-one relationship in most cases. We'll see what the exact value is, but for now, let's say a call option for Apple stock will move in such a way that for every dollar Apple gains and losses, the price of the option will move by $0.80. This is on a per-share basis—so for the option overall, a $1 move in the stock means an $80 move in the option's value.

This cut both ways, so options trading is not for the faint of heart. It also requires discipline. If you are watching an option over a single day, you might see it go up and down by $50 in value if there is a lot of volatility.

However, the advantage is that a small price increase in a stock can quickly lead to big profits. Suppose that you bought that Apple option for $125. If the price per share of Apple goes up to $0.40, then the option's price would rise to $157. Had it gone up to $1, the option would rise in price to $205.

Remember that goes both ways, so a decline in price by 40 cents would drop a $125 option to $93. Option prices can move fast throughout the day, so you have to keep a close eye on it, so you don't get wiped out and take advantage of opportunities to sell for profits.

Each option's price moves concerning the underlying stock price vary depending on the individual option. We will discuss how to figure out the possible price changes later.

Options Have a Higher ROI

The return on investment for an option is much higher than for stocks. Let's say you had $5,000 to invest, and we used that to buy Apple shares at $200 a share. That would give us 25 shares. If the price went up by $2, that would give us a $50 profit, ignoring commissions. So, we'd have an ROI of:

ROI = $50/$5,000 x 100 = 1%

That isn't a bad share increase for a single day move. Investors in stocks are looking for a return of maybe 8% *per year*.

We could buy 40 options contracts at $125 each. The total profit per option contract is $160. Our net profit with $0 commissions on Robinhood would be $6,400. The ROI in the options case is:

ROI = $6,400/$5,000 x 100 = 128%

There are even bigger opportunities than this. On certain days, you'll see stocks make big moves, like after an earnings announcement. The share price could go up to $10 or $20 if earnings beat expectations. The opportunities for profits are enormous.

Options Are Flexible

It's common to talk about call options because it is easier for beginners to understand, but put options give the options trader advantages a stock investor doesn't have. What if instead, the stock price of Apple dropped $2? In that case, the investor in the Apple stock would lose $50 instead. It's not a huge loss to be sure, but a loss is a loss.

However, a clever options trader who saw the decline coming could have bought put options with their money. For the sake of simplicity, assuming that the price of the option was the same and it related to the stock price in the same way, the price of the put options would go up by $6,400 when the price of Apple dropped $2. And we'll see later that you can devise strategies that will earn profits no matter which way the stock price moves. These techniques go by the name of straddle, strangle, and iron condor, among others.

Options Are Fast

Options have an expiration date. Some people will see this as a negative, but others will find it refreshing. Since options have an expiration date, they are not assets that you're going to hold onto very long (except for LEAPS). For those that like an asset with an expiration date, the result of this on a practical level is that with options, you will get in and get out of your trades pretty quickly. You might periodically do day trades when a stock is experiencing large price movements. I typically do 2-3 a week (remember don't do 4 a week unless you plan to deposit $25,000 and accept the day trader designation). In most cases, you'll hold the option for a couple of days and then sell it when the opportunity arises. If you are selling to open, you'll be holding the position anywhere from a week to a month or two, but there is no long-term investing.

Chapter 14. Binary Options Trading

One of the options trading methods that have been very popular in recent times is binary options. While many options traders associated gambling with binary options, it is very clear that many people have little to no knowledge about what binary options are and how to trade them. Today, there are millions of people who trade binary options without an understanding of how it works. They are lured by greed and the desire to make money quickly. While the binary option is a high-risk option trading, many people increase their own risk and blow off their trading capital through their ignorance of the trade. So, the first thing you want to do is to make sure you know what binary options are, where to trade them, and how to trade them.

What Are Binary Options?

Binary options are exotic options whose payoff is based on a "Yes" or "No" predictions. This is the reason it is called binary option: you have only two options for winning, either a "Yes" or a "No." Unlike other options trading methods, you stand a chance to make money when your predictions are right and then you lose the money you invested when your predictions are wrong. It is a "something or nothing at all" type of options trading.

Usually, the binary options of the U.S. offer a fixed monetary return to the trader when the underlying prediction regarding the option is right. In the U.S., binary options are usually traded for a minimum of $100. Non-U.S. traded binary options offer a percentage amount when the predictions are right. The most important factor is to read, analyze, and understand the dangers of working with the binary option before diving into the trade.

Here is a sample scenario dealing with binary options: will the price of an underlying security (gold, silver, stock, index, etc.) be above $ 1,200 by 5 pm?

A binary option for an underlying asset may be trading at a bid price of $ 36 and an offer price of $ 40.00 at 3 pm. If you want to buy the binary option, then you will have to pay an amount of $ 36.00. If you want to sell, then you will sell at $ 40.00.

If the asset's price is above $ 1,200 by 5 pm, the binary option will expire in the money, and you'll be entitled to $ 100.00. Your profit margin will be $ 64 (gain minus cost of binary option). However, if its value never went above $ 1200, the binary option will expire out of the money, and you'll earn $ 0.00.

How to Spot Scam Binary Option Brokers

The world of binary option is full of scams and fraudulent brokers who simply want to make money off investors and novice traders. In fact, there are myriad of stories of people whose funds have been locked with fraud binary options traders who have used seductive schemes to lure people to trade and lose their hard-earned money.

If you want to trade binary options, you have to, first of all, differentiate between the scam brokers from the real ones. If you don't, you'll find yourself being trodden by sharks and wolves. So, how do you spot a scam binary options broker?

Scam Binary Options Software

This is the first scam that many scam binary options brokers use. They say on their website that they have trading software that ensures you make a profit through every trade. You will make consistent wins; all trades are risk-free.

Trading Bonus

They even provide you with a trading bonus to get started with. They claim they provide you with a specific amount of money to get started and test the system for yourself. This lures people to invest with their own money.

Fake Testimonials

They provide you with testimonials of people who have used their scam trading software to make a sum only in a short time. Don't fall for this fraud, all those testimonials are fake.

Huge Deposits

They require you to make a huge deposit with them to use the software to earn money. If you fund your trading account with the money, you'll be absolutely scammed and never be able to access the funds again.

Fund Withdrawal Issues

When you win as they rightly said, you can't withdraw your funds. You can try as hard as you can, but that's not going to work. Their email address can't be accessed. When they realize people know their domain name, they shut down their website and build another one with a new domain name.

Basic Steps for Binary Options Trading

Trading in binary options might be different from other types of options. The most common type is the fixed return option, where you can trade in stocks, indexes, commodities, and currencies. The following are the steps to take to get started in trading in binary options the right way:

1. Select a broker(s)

This is the most important step. You have to choose a broker that is licensed to provide binary options brokerage offers. Skip the scam brokers and look for credible brokers. You can also use multiple brokers. Some of the known binary options brokers are Expert Options, IQ Trading, 24 Option, and Binary Options Auto Trading.

2. Register and make a deposit to start trading

After you have read and analyzed the broker carefully, the next step is to follow the steps outlined to register on the trading platform. By registering, you can now get access to the members-only trading area. This should be followed by making a deposit on the platform to start trading. You need at least $ 100 to get started.

3. Select your asset class and trade type

What do you want to trade? You have to select the asset class: foreign currency, stock, index, commodities, and so forth. Once you're done, you can then determine your trade. There are various types of binary options offered by brokers: high low/call put, one-touch, no-touch, 30 seconds, and boundary options.

4. Determine the amount to invest

How much do you want to invest in the trade? For example, if you're trading high low/call put, you can select call when you think that the price of an underlying asset will rise. If that happens, you will be entitled to win the stated amount for the option. When the never happens, you'll lose. This also applies to put options.

5. Determine your win/loss

The exciting thing about binary options is that you can win hundreds of dollars in a few minutes if your predictions are right. For instance, if your trade has a payout promise of 90% for $ 100 investment, you can stand the chance of winning $ 90 in a short period of time.

But, you can also lose. This is the reason it is advisable to only invest money you can afford to lose in all options, including binary option. Don't get too greedy and dip all your trading capital into a binary options trade. You'll risk being wiped out of the market completely.

Chapter 15. Candlestick Charts and Patterns

Candlestick charts weren't known in the West before the 1980s when they were introduced. However, Japan used this method for centuries, which at the same time makes Japan the place of origin of the candlestick method. As we have already seen before, these charts show the same information as the bar chart that was used in our country's way before we started using the Japanese system. The reason that the candlestick charts became so popular in such a short amount of time is the fact that it is easier to understand and it uses simple yet innovative body illustration that helps the investor seeing every change at a glance.

Let's recap some of the basic characteristics of the candlestick as the general pattern. Firstly, the total length of the candle represents the trading range for the predetermined period. The body of the candle is connected to the distance between the prices known as the closing price and the opening price. The difference in color shows if the price went up or down for a certain period. The length of the candle also portrays the volatility of the price, and the sum of the candle and the "body" of the candle can be viewed as the progress that was made for one day. If the chart shows that the candle's "body" is short, it means that the closing and the opening prices were close or similar. If that is the case, we can say that the buyers and the sellers were in balance.

Types

When it comes to the candlestick chart, we can say that there are regular candles and then that there is Doji. This is a special candle which body is just a horizontal line. This line represents closing prices and opening prices, which in case you have Doji are equivalent.

If the candles have long bodies that will indicate that the trend of the price is strong. If your chart has candles without any wicks, it means that you got Marubozu, which is an indicator that shows that the trades were only made in the range of the opening and closing prices; thus, no trade was made outside of that range. This is a very strong indication, which means that the market was strongly pushing the price only in one direction.

Hammer

When it comes to ideal signals, in Hammer, that signal is represented with a small body. Its wick should be two times longer than the body regardless of the day being up or down for the price trend. Hammer sometimes signals that the trend of the price will reverse. The way to confirm such an assumption and make it actionable is to wait for the following day and see if the price is going to increase. If the price starts rising, it means that your interpretation of trend reversal has been confirmed. This pattern works because of many traders' panic, and if the price is down for some time, they will sell at any price. If we try to express this situation in the candle chart, it means that the wick is going to be pushed down. However, smart investors come in, and they buy, which pushes the price up once again. These trend reversals can last through the whole day and even keep up happening the following day too.

Hanging Man

The Hanging Man is a pattern that looks the same as the Hammer; the only difference is that it comes in an uptrend. Just like before, we search for a change in the price trend on the following day so we could confirm our estimation of the trend's reversal. The psychology, in this case, is that traders mostly decide to take profits. That way, they push the prices down. Still, some of those who are new on the market see this as their chance to buy. That way, they push the price back up. In any case, this candle is considered to be weak. As a reflection of this pattern, it appears that traders have a hunch that this means that the trend is over, so the selling starts to rise again in the following few days.

Inverted Hammer

Once you see the diagrams for the first two candlestick patterns, you will realize that the inverted hammer also has similar characteristics. There is also certain psychology behind its signaling, and we will briefly explain it. Once the downtrend starts weakening and several traders have second thoughts, they start buying, which pushes the prices up. Sellers also come back in the game, which means that the price will close down. However, if the price starts increasing during the following day, then the conclusion is that the weakness of the trend made buyers buying even more while pushing up the prices, and that way, the uptrend started.

Shooting Star

The last but not the least in the set of four related candle signals is the pattern known as the Shooting Star, which comes in an uptrend. Everybody knows that beginners or novices, if you prefer, tend to buy on the top. Shooting star demonstrates simply the exuberance that the future causes the traders to see the high wick that appears when novices enter the market. The traders who notice this are usually those who appeared thinking that it is time to sell. Just like in every other pattern above, the only way to confirm this is to wait up the following day and to determine if that was the signal that shows that the trend will reverse.

Bullish Engulfing

This is a pattern that consists of two candles, and it is graded as highly probable. When in a downtrend, the first candle pressures that the selling continues. The pressure is strong enough to allow the following candle to open up at an even lower price. However, those investors who are smart see an opportunity here, and they start buying on the second candle in this case. This makes the price to grow and launches it above the limit of the preceding period. This is one of the numerous proofs that the real power is in the hands of the buyers, and that there is a high possibility that the trend will reverse.

Bearish Engulfing

It has the same concept as bullish engulfing. The thing is that sometimes uptrend can stretch so badly that the opening price can even go higher than the current price in the earlier candle. Smart and experienced investors usually decide to sell on these occasions. The length of the candle, in this case, shows that the trend can be reversed from an uptrend to a downtrend due to the weight of an opinion.

Piercing Candle

Piercing candle is a pattern that represents a strong bearish candle that is in a downtrend. This candle, with another following candle, opens up at a price that is lower than the current one. However, the candle is rallying to have the finishing price, which has the same trading range as the earlier day. This pattern can be seen as a signal for the trend reversal, and the reason for that is piercing candle as an indicator that sellers are feeling hopeless. When the low prices go even lower, it is an opportunity for those who consider themselves to be smart investors to start buying and to push prices strongly up.

Dark Cloud Cover

This is a pattern that has entirely the same characteristic as the piercing candle pattern. The only difference is that the dark cloud cover is in an uptrend.

Bullish Harami

This pattern has a name that originated from the Japanese word Harami that means "pregnant." As the name suggests, the reason for this is that according to them, these candlestick patterns have a resemblance to the pregnant women. If you happen to encounter the bullish Harami, it means that the market had a lot of active sellers. However, the other candle indicates that the current price became higher. If the second candle finishes up and provides buying enough pressure, you can see it as a signal that there is going to be a change in the price trend. As usual, the following day is a confirmation checker.

Bearish Harami

When a pattern reaches an end of an uptrend, there can be a candle that demonstrates exuberance that some might see as naive. When the other period opens up, and the price is lower continuing to go lower as the day goes by, we can say that it indicates second thoughts in buyers. The most probable income of this situation is that the selling will continue regularly and that everything will be resolved once when the price goes into a downtrend.

Candlestick Pattern Rules

Candlestick patterns named aren't the only one that exists. However, these are the main or the most popular ones that you might find useful during your trading career. Like we mentioned once before, nowadays, numerous programs and servers can calculate, estimate, and identify any pattern that you are interested in. Keep in mind that trading should never be done based on one strategy or just one resource, which is why we wouldn't recommend that you start trading relying only on the information you gather through the candlestick principle, for example. Remember, the validity of the pattern depends on the right trend in which the pattern needs to work in. Also, many other indicators have to be taken into consideration.

Trading Platforms

Options trading platforms come in several varieties. These are offered by brokerage firms to help you trade at any level you want. Some platforms only feature basic components, while others contain more advanced features such as trade and market analytics, as well as pricing tools. These are available as web-based applications or as standalone programs. The decision to use any of these lies with the investor.

Choosing the right options trading platform that suits your needs is very important because it can make your trading experience more productive and less time-consuming. However, with the wide array of platforms available on the market, selecting one that is good can become a tedious exercise. This is because some platforms are more advertised than others.

Price per Trade

This is always the first consideration that investors make when they need to choose a trading platform. The price per trade refers to the amount of cash you will pay for each transaction that you complete on the platform. If you are an active trader, then you will realize how important this is each time you have to part with some fees and commissions. You must check out platforms that charge less for each trade you complete.

Monthly Fees

Some platforms charge investors a monthly service fee. This is always in the form of inactivity and maintenance fees. You need a platform that charges zero monthly maintenance fees, as this will ensure that your investment returns remain at a maximum.

Faster Execution

This is another priority for investors and traders. If you need an account that completes your trades faster, then you must choose a platform that allows you to do this with ease. This is quite important when the options you want to trade in represent fast-moving assets. In this case, the difference between getting a profit and losing your investment lies in how fast your orders are processed. Therefore, the execution speed of transactions should be a top priority for you if you want to succeed in your trades.

Besides the speed, you also want to get a platform that brings added value to you. For instance, some platforms always offer value promotions for their clients. Like when you open an account, you are given $1000 free. Others provide 24/7 user support, while some even offer free research tools. Some platforms also feature demo accounts that allow you to learn the trade before you can start placing orders through your real account.

Chapter 16. Reasons That Options Are Great for Investing

Now that you have gotten a bit of information about these options and how they work, you can understand how some people would love to get into options and use this to make more money. You need to really know the market and be smart with the options that you choose, but options can be a great way to make a lot of money. All this may seem a little complicated and you may wonder why you would want to work with options in the first place. Here are some of the best reasons why you should consider trading with options and adding this investment to your portfolio when you're ready to make some good money:

Options Are Flexible

When you're working with options, you'll find that you get a ton of flexibility. You can choose to buy or sell, you can go with different expiration dates, you can pick from a variety of strategies and assets, and you can even have control over your strike price. There are even ways that you will be able to profit if the market goes down. Sometimes all this flexibility is going to make working in options more complicated, but if you know what you're doing, this type of flexibility will help you to profit, regardless of how the market is doing.

Lower Startup Costs

Some people find that it's hard to start investing in the stock market because it's so expensive to purchase anything. When you're working with the options market, you're able to make money even with a low investment.

Gain Leverage

Another benefit you get when you decide to work with the options market is the idea of leverage. To keep things simple, leverage is a big advantage to the trader. When you gain advantage, you are giving yourself more options because you're able to put more money into the market without needing to have more startup capital to help you out. This can be dangerous because it causes you to lose more money than you have in the beginning, but if you're careful and read the market right, it will make you earn a ton more money even with lower startup costs.

Low Risk

You will find that working with options can be relatively low risk. First, these options are more affordable than what you're able to get with some other types of investing, so you're limiting the risks that you're taking, as long as you use the right strategies as you do it. You can even look at some of the trades and pick the ones that have less risk so that you will lose less, even if the trade doesn't go the way that you want.

Lots of Benefits

If you are used to working in the stock market, you will find that trading in options can have more benefits. To start, options trading is often more profitable than trading in the stock market. A small movement with traditional stocks can affect your investment a ton, something that doesn't happen when you're working with options.

Limit Your Risk

A good reason to go with buying options is that you'll be able to limit your risk down to just the amount of money that you pay for the premium. With other investment options, you could end up losing a lot of money, even money that you did not invest to begin with, but this does not happen when you're working with options.

Let's say that you saw that the prices of cows were about to go up. You could pay some money upfront and enter a contract with someone else to sell your five cows for $2000. At this point, since you're working with an options contract, you did not buy the cows upfront.

On the other hand, if you had gone up to the other person and purchased those cows straight up for a cost of $10,000, you could end up in trouble. For this example, the price of the cows may end up falling by $500, rather than going up by $500, and you would end up losing $2500 in the process. Since you went into the options contract, you would stand to lose no more than $250 if the prices were to fall afterwards. You still stand to lose some money, but it's a lot less than you would have lost otherwise.

Better Leverage for the Money

You will find that when you're working with options it can provide you with some good leveraging power. A trader will be able to buy an option position that will imitate their stock position quite a bit, but it will end up saving them a lot of money in the process.

Let's say you have an opportunity to make a profitable trade, you can only spare about $1000 to purchase the stock, but you don't know options are available. If we were still talking about the cows from before, you would not be able to purchase even one cow for the money (remember that they are about $2000 each without the options contract), and so you would completely miss out on the possibility to make a profit.

However, if you decided to purchase with an options contract, rather than purchasing the underlying asset outright, the dynamics have completely changed. This could result in an investment of just $250 to get started. The premium on the options contract is a fraction of the total cost, allowing you to get in on the trade for a lot less money. If you watch options contracts, you will be able to make more purchases, and potentially more money, compared to some of the other stock choices you can make.

Higher Percentage of Returns

As mentioned, an options trader is only going to pay a fraction of the value of the asset just to have some control over that asset. This will allow the trader to earn more money than what they would be able to earn when they purchase the asset upfront and then try to sell it. Let's take a look at an example of how this can work.

Going back to the idea of the cows, the market price at the beginning of this trade is $2000. For a regular cattle trader, one who doesn't know anything about options, had the $2000 in hand and believed that the price of the cattle is going to go up, he would only have the opportunity to purchase on cow. If the price of the cows goes up to $2500, this trader will only be able to make a profit of $500. This isn't bad, but since it presents a big risk here, it isn't always the best.

On the other hand, a trader who knows a bit about options will be able to do things a bit different. If you had $2000, you could choose to purchase eight options contracts, with a premium of $50. This means that you now have the purchasing rights for a total of 40 cows rather than the 1 cow the other trader had.

With the same profit of $500 per cow, your profit would be $18,000 (this includes the $500 per cow minus the $2000 you spent in the beginning to purchase the contracts). You earned thousands of dollars more compared to the original trader, but you used the same amount of money to get started.

Helps to Hedge Intraday or Futures Trades

It is common for traders to purchase or short-sell Futures contracts because they expect them to move in one direction or another. Intraday traders may do the same thing, because they will purchase many shares in the hopes that they will move down or up during that day. If the trader ends up picking the wrong direction on the Futures or the intraday trades, they may end up losing a lot of weight. Unless you put in a stop-loss, there is the probability to lose an unlimited amount of money in the process.

You may not be complaining when this goes the right way and you earn unlimited profits, but if you go with one of these trades and you don't hedge your position, you will complain when you start losing a lot of money. If you have an understanding of how trading options works, you could buy call or put options to help ensure that you aren't going to end up with an unlimited loss. The right options choice is going to help control your loss the moment that the intraday or futures positions start going against what you wanted.

While there are a lot of great investment choices that you can make, none of them will limit your risk as much as options while still providing you with a great potential to make money in the process. This is a great investment for anyone, whether they are just getting started with investing or they have been in the market for a long time.

Conclusion

You are at the end of the book: Options Trading for Beginners Book Outline and thank you for reading through it and making it to the end. Let's be hopeful that it has been helpful enough to provide the knowledge and skills that are needed to start trading in options as a newbie in the market. As not everything might have been covered in this book outline, it would also be great if you would seek to enrich yourself with such knowledge from other sources apart from this book. The book has nonetheless covered great subjects on the introduction of the options market to a new and a beginner trader that seeks to apprentice the reader to the market. Written in this outline, as you've read, is a comprehensive guide to starting trading in options.

It also piques up your interest to find more about options trading and how they operate in making money. You are also encouraged to start on trading options by the book outlining the advantages of the trade that leaves you motivated to start on it already. You are made aware of the fundamentals of the trade and the components of it, further expanding your knowledge of the options market, which will prove to be very helpful to a beginner in the market, for they are well aware of what options trading comprises of.

The highlight of the book to the reader is talking about how to get started in trading the options. This part offers you the practical skills and gears you up to take the first step in making your beginner trade. The knowledge written in this book would be to naught if you, the reader, who is a beginner trader, would not make the first trade, following care guidelines. And this book has just done that. Written down great and helpful tactics to kick you off as you start your journey in the options trading world. After gaining such skills, employ them in the real market world and get to experience the highs and the lows, but as stated in the book, nonetheless great strategies.

As a beginner in trading, you have also benefited from other aspects written in the book such as risk and risk management; very crucial, leverage, and others such as technical analysis. These aspects will be vital in trading, for in most cases that determine the profitability of the trades that you have made. Let's hope that you have gone through these aspects carefully and taken away the key points that will be crucial when you are trading. Factors such as leverage will distinguish you from becoming a professional trader in no time and a trader who makes mistakes and errors that would have otherwise been avoided. As observed in the book, it can be termed as the backbone that holds the trading. It is the most important takeaway you can take. Without the analysis, your takeoff as a beginner trader would be baseless, for you would be making assumptions on the market without any reference, which is a suicidal thing to do in the market.

Of great import to traders in this book outline as they progress from being beginners is the subject of psychology in trading. We are hopeful that you will be able to learn from this outline the importance of trading with your emotions kept in check, as the book advertises, for successful trading. Apply this knowledge in real-time trading and approach the market in the right mental state, this being one of the skills that were mentioned in the psychology of options trading.

As a beginner, probably the most exciting part of the book was where tips on succeeding in options trading were extensively written down. This should buoy your beginner trading spirits up and gear you up for being successful in this field, which you'll be, after following the tips outlined here and from many other sources. To be fully confident in your trading capacities and abilities, this outline had also provided in text form of the mistakes that are to be avoided when you are trading.

All this said, it remains up to you, the beginner reader of trading in options to make the most crucial move; and that is making your first trade. This should not be procrastinated as the book has prepared you enough for the market, and you should be confident to make trades and make it a learning experience from your gains and losses, which are a sure thing to make in trading. Also, be sure to get useful information from enlightening sources to keep you on top-notch. We hope the skills that you've gathered from this awesome book will prove to be helpful as you start trading and making your way in options trading. We wish you the best of luck as you start on this enthralling endeavor in your life, packed with all the information you need. May you make the best trades and predictions with this outline as your guiding ray.

www.ingramcontent.com/pod-product-compliance
Lightning Source LLC
Chambersburg PA
CBHW070350220526
45467CB00001B/316